Rant

RANT

Emigre No. 64

❋❋❋❋❋❋❋❋❋❋❋❋❋

WINTER 2003

Co-published by
PRINCETON ARCHITECTURAL PRESS

Edited and designed by Rudy VanderLans.
Copy editing by Alice Polesky.

Emigre, 4475 D Street, Sacramento, California 95819
Visit our web site at www.emigre.com.

Co-published by Princeton Architectural Press
37 East Seventh Street
New York, New York 10003
For a free catalog of books, call 1.800.722.6657.
Visit our Web site at www.papress.com.

Printed and bound in the USA in an edition of 6,000 copies.

06 05 04 03 5 4 3 2 1 First edition

ISBN 1-56898-409-X
ISSN 1045-3717

FOR *Graphic* DESIGNERS

CONTENTS

AFTER ABOUT TEN ISSUES OR so filled with visual and aural indulgences, I felt it was time for *Emigre* to return to publishing design criticism and theory. This is a particularly opportune time to do so, I believe, because today there is a plurality of new design styles prevalent in the world which seem to exist independently of local color and ideology, and are largely concerned with how things look, and this has generated no opposition or in-depth critique. In general, I've noticed a lack of critical investigation into today's graphic design scene, with few, if any, new voices writing passionately about graphic design.

One trend in question stands out and needs scrutiny. On the surface it seems to be a reaction to 90s personal expressionism. It is epitomized by a return to Helvetica – and all its bland cousins, nieces and nephews – and it employs simple systems, modules, and grids to replace ideas. Typographically, it looks something like this:

BLAHBLAHBLAH
BLAHBLAHBLAHBLAHBLAHBLAH

001: BLAH BLAH BLAH	**010: BLAH BLAH BLAH**
002: BLAH BLAH BLAH	**011: BLAH BLAH BLAH**
003: BLAH BLAH BLAH	**012: BLAH BLAH BLAH**
004: BLAH BLAH BLAH	**013: BLAH BLAH BLAH**
005: BLAH BLAH BLAH	**014: BLAH BLAH BLAH**
006: BLAH BLAH BLAH	**015: BLAH BLAH BLAH**
007: BLAH BLAH BLAH	**016: BLAH BLAH BLAH**
008: BLAH BLAH BLAH	**017: BLAH BLAH BLAH**
009: BLAH BLAH BLAH	**018: BLAH BLAH BLAH** etc.

There are many other features associated with this new style, such as vector-based, silhouetted illustrations — sometimes filled with gradated colors — or the obviously computer generated and seemingly-self-mutating-polygon-architectural-3D-photo-collages, or the high-contrast images reminiscent of Che Guevara's well-known portrait. Another trend is the ubiquitous toddler-like cartoon creatures with big heads that look at you with even bigger eyes and always seem to be asking: "Don't you love me?" I don't understand what that's all about. Answers about the how and why of these new mannerisms are nowhere to be found, or at least I couldn't find them. It is as if they just dropped to earth from outer space, which they obviously didn't because typographically much of it looks an awful lot like what Walter Herdig's *Graphis* magazine used to publish in the early 60s, except for those big-eyed creatures. Those are just weird.

There are many styles floating around today, and with most designs it is easy to determine which approach the designer is trying to emulate. It is as if graphic designers all work from the same palette; a broad but finite set of mannerisms that are often applied willy-nilly without any conviction other than a solid belief in good taste. Some designers think this is what graphic design is all about. Like style merchants, they pick and choose from what is currently hip and readily acceptable to infuse the work of their clients with a dose of contemporary cool.

THERE'S LITTLE YOU CAN DO about design styles. They come and go. And sometimes they come back again. But I'm always curious. Where do styles originate? How do they evolve, and why? What do they signify? How does style affect the way we represent and interpret the world? These are some of the issues that design criticism and theory address. However, the road to criticism is littered with the cadavers of failed magazines. Investigations into the deeper meaning of graphic design are dismissed by most designers as non-essential, ineffectual, and not pertinent to the everyday reality of what it means to be a practicing graphic designer.

This has always baffled me.

Satisfying customers, solving problems, and bringing home a paycheck are noble pursuits, even essential. But what sets graphic design apart from many other professions is how it adds value beyond utility and profits – how it differentiates and mediates our messages while enriching our visual culture. Design criticism probes these aspects. As a graphic designer, how can you not be interested in this?

I'm aware that publishing design criticism and theory may seem even more irrelevant at a time when many graphic designers are struggling to make ends meet. It's difficult to question and investigate the deeper meaning of design when you have a hard time finding work. Yet maybe the reason we are in a creative and economic slump is due in part to a lack of any serious or sustained criticism when it mattered most, when we were flying high. The excesses of the late 90s were bound to come to an end. Not so, we were told. We were at the dawn of a new era. This was a new economy. Or so the news media told us. Instead of questioning, everybody crowded around the trough.

So, too, did graphic design and advertising. Around the turn of the century, it was happily aiding and abetting the culture of decadence, splurging with XL designer monographs, extravagant design conferences, luxurious bi-coastal design offices, and paper company promotions crowding out design magazine editorials. When money is flush, when things are moving along just fine, why bother asking difficult questions? Why upset the status quo? That's why the First Things

First manifesto 2000 rubbed so many graphic designers the wrong way.

So apparently, there is never a right time for criticism. We are either too busy making money, or too miserable for lack of it. Plus, according to recent sentiments, to criticize is to be against (you're either with us, or against us).

Nothing could be further from the truth. To criticize, one could argue, is to care to an extreme extent. Criticism investigates our actions and motivations, and can provide new insights into what we take for granted. It can alert us to stagnation, question unfounded claims, and place our work in a larger social, historical, and cultural context. It is born from an innate need to ask "Why?" Of course, criticism has many limitations. It can never replace the work it addresses, and cannot exist without it. So graphic designers need not fear it.

EMIGRE, AND THE WORK WE PUBLISHED, was itself the object of much criticism in the early 90s. Most of it came from an older generation. I remember how exciting it was to have these men discuss our work. It had obviously made an impression on them; enough to get them riled. Cranky old guys, we thought they were. But it could not be denied; these men were passionate about graphic design. They could not resist pointing out what they thought was lacking in our work. And we, in turn, could not stop ourselves from firing back, explaining our motives and questioning theirs. The results were at times insightful, dreadfully boring, inspiring, sometimes grossly uninformed, but always impassioned. And the discourse played out over a number of years in magazines like *Eye*, the *AIGA Journal* and *Emigre*. This period, unfortunately labeled as "The Legibility Wars," generated one of the most prolific investigations into graphic design seen to date.

How to bring back the excitement? Perhaps it's *Emigre*'s turn to become the voice of cranky old designers. Instead of waiting for a new generation to fan the flames and bring back the passion, maybe it is our professional responsibility to speak up and point out what we feel is lacking in graphic design today. Maybe it is even expected of us, like a pecking order thing.

And thus the idea for *Emigre* No. 64 was born. Taking our cue from the cranky old men of the 90s, we invited a number of long-time *Emigre* contributors to rant about the state of graphic design in 2002. The idea was to generate a critique of today's design scene, a provocation of sorts, a passionate kick in the knees. The Legibility Wars of the 90s exposed the intentions and ambitions of graphic designers with widely divergent viewpoints. I'm sure everybody learned something from the experience. At the very least, it showed us that graphic design is not just about solving clients' problems. With this issue, we hope to rekindle the discussion.

Rudy VanderLans

Quietude

By Kenneth FitzGerald

It's a pretty, subdued time in design. Passions are running low—or are highly affected. Design continues to be a busy but overly placid, pleasant surface. There are few signs of what, if anything, lies below that surface. Our pond remains small and shallow. Anyone hoping for waves is waiting for someone else to make them.

There was some disturbance but the breakers seem to have settled out—and settled in. Have we arrived at a transition or a terminus? A breather or an expiration? A perpetual revolution (if that's what it was) is tough to maintain. Design might be process but there needs be a product. What have we produced?

That nonconformist forms were readily absorbed into the mainstream shouldn't have come as a surprise. It's the life cycle of style. The once-rebellious designers who have joined the establishment are not necessarily hypocrites. Often, that label was applied by the established. Cooption is natural, though humdrum.

The rhetoric—and the work—of the past decade did get overheated. But design actually ran a temperature for a time. Now, the field has resumed its disdain for passion. Due either to remnants of Modern objectivity or to professional control, ADs insist on an AC heart.

With heat came light. Design mattered, as it hadn't before. Or it mattered to me, who had previously dismissed it. What was exciting about the striking work is that it accompanied an intellectual agitation. It struck matches, not just eyes. And it's that adventure—that promise—which has gone missing.

Present and accounted for is a lot of sumptuous work that follows routes charted during the ferment. It's also everywhere: both on diverse and unexpected artifacts and wherever there's a design industry. A curious realization of the Modern dream—a cross-country, cultural language of form—continues to be fulfilled. Only in our here-and-now, that language is appropriated, not apprehended.

If æsthetically pleasing product is what design's all about, things are good. However, the call that cut across all the strata of discourse was that design needed some meaning. A content of its own. And that perpetual longing: respect as a substantive activity.

A permanent insurrection is an impossible brief. Somewhere along the line, though, victory seems to have been declared. Or the battle map was redrawn. A dialogue "daisy-cutter" hit and sucked all the oxygen out of our cave. Design was supposed to surge from this dark Platonic netherworld. It must have been too bright out there, since we've all ducked back into the studio. The illumination is evidently better from those expensive light booths. Enough talk, that was fun—back to work!

If you won't take my word for it, take Rick Poynor's. He's still prodding design to allow for a real criticism. With his insistence that design is worthy of an accessible, expansive, sustained, and discerning inquiry (articulated recently in *Print*), he may be the person who most believes in design. His provocations for a critical journalism are *Theses* nailed on design's front door.

Sadly, no one's reading them. Maybe he doesn't use enough imagery or needs to do his own typography for design to notice. I admire Poynor's optimism and persistence. I've simply given up on a critical writing ever developing in the design field. If it evolves, it will be from the outside, likely an aspect of the ongoing hybridization of media. Also, art may continue to drift into design in its slow absorption of all cultural production.

That would be unfortunate, as design writing could take what's best about art criticism—its intellectual rigor—and inject social and cultural relevance. It could also squelch its ardor for architecture's status and theory. Both art and architecture are overwrought and value megalomania, excessive capital, and grandiosity. ("Oh, Rem, it's so big!")

The demise of discourse is due to neglect. Designers vote with their eyes and look away. And there isn't much to look away from. No market exists for critical writing. The major publications know what their audience wants—and it's not criticism. The desired report is brief, written by a professional and professionally oriented. Anything of subtlety, depth, and breadth is ignored. Profiling a designer with some connection to celebrity and capital prevails over a think piece every time.

The passing of the intellectually tepid *Critique* symbolizes design's disinterest in anything approaching inquiry. Only the pretense of deeper readings exists in current magazines. The *AIGA Journal* transformed itself into the bookish *Trace* (now defunct) but its articles remained mostly trivia. The fussy, homogenizing design displayed detailed photographs of various mundane objects as if promising a similarly methodical examination of design issues. Instead, both only addressed the surface. Engagement with any serious topics were left to (surprise!) Rick Poynor or the token profiled fine artist.

Eye magazine seems to have read the lack of writing on the wall. It has faded from intellectually vital to commercially demonstrative. An aggressive marketing campaign and a busy layout attempts to fill the void left after the departure of its founding editor and his successor. Quantity reigns over quality of the contributors and the reviews. It's heartening that *Eye* is featuring lesser or unheard voices. So far, the newer writers are indistinct and the product often immaterial.

Meanwhile, many well known design voices are now making

it full-time. As in art, design's practitioners/writers prefer the former role. It's a problem for design when just a few people leave the field and a chasm opens. This intensifies the need for design to develop an independent body of critical writers. That still doesn't exist and the potential is dim. In the twilight, design continues to evade any substantive internal critique. If you're a designer with a book and haven't been overly contumelious, you're good to gold.

Design has no heritage of or belief in criticism. Design education programs continue to emphasize visual articulation, not verbal or written. The goal is to sell your idea to a client and/or a hypothetical audience. Design in relation to culture and society is rarely confronted.

There are also some all-too-human dimensions. Design is still a small, small world. Friends are often writing about friends. While design isn't alone or first in closed-circuit critiques, it's there. Even when writers I respect discuss designers I admire, I wonder what a less connected account might offer. That said, the paucity of critics means that fewer articles would be written if we limited such connections.

In addition, there's professional courtesy. You don't dis your peers. Sharing a dais on the next stop in the design conference round robins might get a tad uncomfortable. And since the outside world doesn't take us too seriously, we must stick together, right?

The insularity only reinforces the indifference to design outside its own borders. And even if that's true, it's not the real problem. Luminaries desire an imprimatur. Instead of enlisting critics on the order of Hal Foster or Dave Hickey, sympathetic insiders are tapped. Why not? It's bad business to cast doubt on your talents in your own book. Whatever the rhetoric, design monographs are promotions, period. Client testimonials continue to serve as substantiation. Though we've seen a shift from

CEOs to progressive musicians or philosophers, critical intent is absent.

It's arguable that many of these books are undeserved. We cook a microwave history by beaming intense eminence on excellent but short-careered designers. What nuking does to your leftovers, it does to the quality of scrutiny: scorched on the surface, half-baked to partially-crystallized inside. It's ultimately irrelevant if attention is unmerited. I don't have to buy the book. Unfortunately, with design's failure to commission critical audits, the market is the only check on hype inflation.

Despite the brief and ironic "No More Heroes" movement (more twitch than movement, really), design craves celebrities. Stoking the desire is the publishing industry's need for product. Magazine pages must be filled; books must spew from the pipeline. To move them, the blurb and inside text better gush, too.

OUR CURRENT QUAALUDE INTERLUDE has served to inflate the size of the volumes and the praise for their producers. Against a featureless background, every detail magnifies in enormity. It's not enough to be an exceptional designer; you must be a latter-day Geoffrey Tory with the contemporary sociological acumen of a Marshall McLuhan, or a virtual one-man Bauhaus complete with their self-promotional vigor.

Recent design monographs reveal what the field values. Also on view are themes endemic to design: the rationalization of personal indulgence into a societal benefit, that mimesis is comparable to creation, gesture can substitute for action, formal facility proves conceptual acuity, and popularity equals profundity.

Leo Lionni crafted an unintentional fable of design in his children's book *A Color of His Own*. In it, a chameleon despairs of ever gaining a distinct and stable identity, as he is forced to blend into his environment. Graphic designers often display similar crises and adopt the mien of their clientele. Often, they go them one worse. Corporate designers deport themselves as ultra-businessmen. Graphic roadies of pop musicians style themselves rock stars.

Bruce Mau clearly wants *Life Style* to rest comfortably amongst the high-culture works he regularly collaborates on. Mau is an outstanding designer, valuable for his exacting craft, and for being unapologetically intellectual. *Life Style* is welcome just so it can be dropped on the massed digits of design's "I think with my hands" crowd.

In comparison to other high brow titles, Mau's designs for Zone Books leap out as vibrant, enticing artifacts. However, for all the talk of serendipitous, experimental, content-driven and contained design, Mau exhibits a formulaic approach to his productions, no matter the medium or forum. As he keeps to a narrow range of clientele, his strategies (restrained typographic pallet, appropriated imagery—usually from fine art and technology, exhaustive reproduction/documentation, abecedaria and indices) may be repeated appropriately. Mau does ask authors and editors to accept more design than they're used to. But while introducing some imaginative and expressive aspects to a staid genre, Mau hardly violates classical conventions. Rather than expanding the role of design-as-livery, his productions are like finely tailored, stylish suits.

Life Style is enlightening when it directly addresses design. Mau's conceptualizing on culture, though, is discomfiting. His writing is far less adapt than his form giving; he adopts his patrons' sweeping generalities and abstruse prose. The majority of concepts that Mau engages have been in play for many years amongst media theorists. His engagement with and restatement of these themes are germane. But a sense of *déjà vu* hovers over the book as similar or identical images and ideas encountered in books such as *Perverse Optimist* and *Pure Fuel* reappear.

The central notion that's unique to Mau is design's need to reclaim a substantial, empowering meaning for the term "life style." Instead of resisting the common depiction of design as a styling process, Mau embraces it. However, his "style" isn't superficial: it's a positive, life-generating operation. Mau hastens through his argument in a few brief and recondite paragraphs then dashes off to other theories. How this new life styling practically differs from the old isn't explained. We can only assume that Mau (and by extension his clients) practices the virtuous version.

Mau links his proposal with Guy Debord and the Situationists to provide it with a radical, anti-capitalist attitude. The inversion is obviously alluring for designers as it converts stigma to sheen simply by proclamation. But absent a proof, it's wishful thinking. The authority for Mau's position apparently rests with his having worked on books like *The Society of the Spectacle*. However meritorious the design—or having read or published the book—such contact doesn't inoculate the principals.

Rather than being "gutted of meaning" in Mau's estimation, the notion of "life style" was hollow from the start. The term deserves disdain because it ultimately bases fulfillment on consumption. You are what you own, not what you do. Designers are complicit in this process, as they regularly craft veneers of "status value" for products.

Mau and his clientele produce commodities uncertain in use value but high in status. Their own consumption and life styling—lusciously detailed in relentlessly name-dropping "Life Stories" sections throughout the book—is privileged and conspicuous. Redefining the term "life style" becomes imperative, as their behavior is materially identical to one Mau labels "vacuous." His life style allows you to indulge in and consume surfaces (Mau acknowledges his reputation was established by his formal innovation), while asserting you're actually involved in a "philosophic project of the deepest order." You can debate which cover of *Life Style* you fancy without feeling shallow.

Rationalizing your activity as critically acute while servicing privileged interests takes an agility that may be appreciated but not encouraged. Mau is hardly alone here. That our valued practitioners inexorably gravitate toward monied culture—fashion, architecture, high art establishments, *etc.* – shows their absolute priority: who can best bankroll my career aspirations? That Mau found a rewarding practice within the jet-set intelligentsia is his good fortune. Offering it as a cultural imperative is something else entirely.

Life Style suggests a critical statement on the "global image economy" but one never materializes. Mau presents it as a spontaneously generated phenomenon which we should "exploit" with "critical engagement." No guidelines are given for what critical engagement is or which design feeds the "downside" of our cultural situation. What we do know is that *Life Style* is surfeited with repurposed imagery and lists at $75.

Life Style is another design spectacle and status asset—a fashion accouterment like the Rem Koolhaas collaboration *S, M, L, XL*. Mau unintentionally confirms this by twice including a photo of that book being used as a pillow. The image falls flat as wry irony or self-deprication. *Life Style* is for and about designers realizing their most grandiloquent contrivances without guilt. The ecological, economic and cultural impact of every similarly motivated artist, designer, or architect pursuing such dreams goes unexamined. Spending $25,000 to reprint a book cover (or having alternate ones) can be regarded either as a "heroic enlargement of work to an ethics" or flagrantly wasting resources. Yes, it happens in design every day. But what is *détournement* without a difference?

DESIGN LOVES ATTESTATION of its heroes and ideology. When designers bring in celebrities to testify to design's import, both get extra credit. Preeminent people who walk into our temple on their own to kneel at the shrine receive our full attention—even when they have little to say. John Maeda puts forth his beliefs simply, pleasantly, and earnestly. Under the ægis of his position at MIT's Media Lab, they play as objective, scientific truth. In its titling, *Maeda on Media* says he is media. However, for someone touted as a seer, Maeda is a curious throwback to simplistic motifs on art, design, and technology popularized decades ago. Those themes are duplicates of Maeda's intellectual and formal mentor, Paul Rand.

Maeda on Media is the book equivalent of a Hollywood blockbuster: long on special effects, short on characterization. The special effects are somewhat tedious. Maeda utilizes the computer exclusively as a pattern-making device. When used insightfully, repetition can have a deep emotional resonance (hear Steve Reich and Philip Glass). Maeda has the instrument but not the sensibility. His design work is acceptable but undistinguished, adorned with variants of warped grids and default sans serif typography. Rather than announcing new directions, they evince nostalgia.

Maeda's achievement may be injecting sentimentality into the "neutral" grid. Neither his generic printed work nor his derivative conceptualizing offers anything for the cultural artifact that is design. His insights on technology never rise above platitudes. To illustrate the computer's emotive potential, Maeda musters sterile, programmed ornamentation. His posting at MIT speaks more to the Media Lab's inbreeding and comfort with hardware, than an ease with and perception of culture. The witty, visually delightful, and politically trenchant work of Amy Franceschini and Josh On of Futurefarmers proposes far more for digital media when it is in the hands of enthusiasts.

GRAPHIC DESIGN LOVES INSPIRATIONAL GUIDES. Case-study tutorials clog the bookstore shelves, most asserting (despite claims to the contrary) that design innovation is reducible to a formal recipe. Even the ostensive monograph frequently turns to delineating how its subject reaches apotheosis, so that others may follow. It is an eccentric conceit of the field that ultimately condescends to its audience. In art, such documents are either obvious parodies or of the *American Artist* ilk.

At 1064 pages, Alan Fletcher's *The Art of Looking Sideways* is design's most massive self-help book yet. The author seems to recognize the messy, transcendent dynamic of inspiration—yet is still moved to represent it in print. To elude this conceptual paradox, he adopts a formless approach. The book is a data-dump of quotations, aphorisms, diagrams, reproductions, commentaries, and folderol. Excess is evidently success.

The patronizing aspect is Fletcher's assumption of massive illiteracy amongst designers. He obviously believes the average practitioner's ignorance could not only fill a book but necessitates one as thick as a cinderblock. The professional blinders widely sported in the field can be maddening, and a broader awareness would benefit design. However, *The Art of Looking Sideways* seems a wild overcompensation. In its enormity—a one-stop cultural supermarket—it suppresses, rather than encourages, individual exploration.

The book's underlying concept, dressed in bang-up graphics, is hoary: inspiration should result from mere exposure to great art, music, or texts. The selected stimuli in *The Art of Looking Sideways* are of the customary motivational genre, presented as one size fits all. The lack of concrete contextualization—how any of this material practically performed in Fletcher's work, or may in anyone else's—makes the choices arbitrary. They function the same as incantations.

Successful people frequently burnish their image. Some elite designers, casting off the stereotype of glorified ad men, posture as scholar-artists. They abstract their process as pursuit of an intellectual purity unaffected by mundanities like clients or careering. Creative genius is all. It is both egotistical and disingenuous to proffer such a selective construct. Though unstated, that's the premise of *The Art of Looking Sideways*, as its existence rests entirely on the author's reputation.

Erudite designers abound (though many are in hiding). A thousand books as worthy as *The Art of Looking Sideways* could be produced. Will Phaidon publish every one? Or, like Alan Fletcher, will the authors need to commission themselves?

IN HIS RECENT BOOK *Fast Food Nation*, Eric Schlosser profiles flavorists—a discreet group of chemist/artists who design the taste of most foods. Their intervention is necessary, as processing destroys inherent taste. Using "natural" and "artificial" flavorings (the definitions are slippery), the flavorists graft a taste onto the food. Schlosser points out that it's just as easy to make your burger taste like cut grass or body odor as it does beef. Graphic designers are often flavorists of print. They inject a factitious aspect of attraction to achieve the natural. Interest can be synthesized and applied indiscriminately to anything.

Stefan Sagmeister's *Made You Look* could bear the title *Every Trick In My Book*. The monograph is a fatiguing compendium of almost every optical, production and advertising-creative artifice devised since Gutenberg. By deploying nearly every special effect (he refrains from die cuts, possibly as a show of restraint), the pages are full-bleed with desperation to clutch a reader's attention. As the audience is designers, Sagmeister knows they're here for a rush. Boisterous pieces set within a hyperactive presentation make *Made You Look* pure designer crack.

As it promises, the book is "...a traditional show-and-tell

graphic design book. No revolutions or big theories in here." So begins a running thread of commentaries marshaled to deflect every attempt to probe beneath any of the surfaces. In its infinite regress of self-referential feints, *Made You Look* is graphic design's *A Heartbreaking Work of Staggering Genius*. Both authors wield formidable technical skills to ingratiate and distract from their meager stories.

Sagmeister is a self-proclaimed, old school "big idea" designer. If there's an analog to which he's digital, it's Bob Gill. Sagmeister prides himself on his professionalism, supposing that it's at odds with the image induced by his graphic products. His "STYLE = FART" motto alleges a position of conceptual prepotency over formal-driven practitioners like David Carson and Neville Brody. In the role of Exposition Man, writer Peter Hall also credits Sagmeister with initiating a "...turning point for the design profession, away from aspirations of digital perfection toward a higher appreciation for a designer's personal mark."

As with other claims of Sagmeister as innovator, this is creditable only if specified to the point of being meaningless. Designers' scrawls are common, and Ed Fella's have proven far more influential and individual. Art Chantry crafts completely hand-made work and has been on the scene far longer. And April Greiman flashed us in the mid-80s. There are numerous signifiers of "personal" in *Made You Look* but nothing that is unmasterly or that disturbs the membrane of professional detachment. The emotional exposure is in inverse proportion to the amount of flaunted skin.

Sagmeister is naughty by nature—never transgressive. The big ideas are frequently obvious or hackneyed metaphors tweaking mainstream taste. That their visualization delivers a jolt points up the timidity of most design. Though Sagmeister doesn't promote a signature formal style, his reliance on visual joy-buzzers becomes style in its own right.

His hanging with rockers and the burgeoning back-to-business mentality in design fueled Sagmeister's notoriety. It is his disconnection that endears him to his primary clientele—and the design profession. Rather than exhibiting the demeanor of a "creative crazy person," Sagmeister's work is always controlled and separated from the raw and real. Rock stars must also affect emotion every night on stage and synthesize it piecemeal and repetitively in the studio. Musicians like the Rolling Stones and Lou Reed are consummate showmen who understand the veneer of passion and getting the job done. Sagmeister fits their bills. And he is completely deferential to his clients' wishes—no artiste tantrums here.

His AIGA Detroit poster, where the copy is etched onto his chest, is a signature work. The image is another stratagem that mocks what it purportedly honors. Sagmeister literally only scratches the surface—he'll itch for his art. The box of Band-Aids he grasps is a stagey wink to us: this is only a graphic design. It's a contrivance artificial as anything spawned through software. Supposedly, the image compels because it shows the maker's hand and provokes an "equally physical response." However, an intern was pressed into service to etch the carefully placed, calligraphed marks when Sagmeister balks at cutting himself. The cojones thrust into our face in the book *Whereishere* are for display only.

The heartbreaking aspect of *Made You Look* is the designer's plaintive quest to answer the question "Can graphic design touch someone's heart?" Curiously placed last on a "To Do" list, it's presented as another career aspiration, not a moral absolute. The structure of the question undermines its answering, stipulating medium before effect. It's the difference between having an idea expressed graphically and a graphic design idea. Sagmeister excels at the latter: his concepts grow out of established graphic design expressions. As such, those conventions will always be in the foreground, like a label stating "artificial flavoring." Shortening the question to "Can I touch someone?" may be the needed natural ingredient.

All art and design is a known construct. We may examine the most disturbing imagery because we know it's false. The most affecting work suspends or interrupts that awareness. Sagmeister's virtuosity is his greatest obstacle. He is constantly pulling his own curtains aside so we may view the machinations of illusion.

The relentless questioning of his work's affectiveness while asserting its effectiveness makes Sagmeister and *Made You Look* schizophrenic. Talking passion is hip; exhibiting it uncool. Are the works he rates as "1s" in the index examples of "touching design"? Or does having his "touching" essay be the book's coda —and going on a highly-touted sabbatical—mean he considers all his designs to this point crowd-pleasing failures? (If meant as a purge, the book makes a lot more sense.) Or, as is often the case with graphic designers, is he trying to have it both ways?

Usually, an expressed desire to do touching work means the same ol' design—but for a high-profile charity. Sagmeister's talent is such that we should hope he finds The Way rather than just a United Way.

THERE HAVE ALSO BEEN MONOGRAPHS that indicate healthy routes to a criticism. Rick Poynor's study of Vaughn Oliver, *Visceral Pleasures*, is a lucid and stimulating text. It establishes Oliver as a rare designer by the quality of his work and willingness to undergo this analysis. Poynor argued for, and received, a restrained presentation from Oliver for the book. While the approach is arguable even if one doesn't require graphic fireworks—does restraint actually allow an objective, considered view or does it adhere to a convention of seriousness?—the resulting book is a powerful convincer, as it should be. At the very least, it's a refreshing respite from overstimulated—and ultimately insecure—offerings like *Made You Look*. Vaughn Oliver may be the one contemporary designer with the right to proclaim himself a fucking genius. *Visceral Pleasures* also proves he's the bravest.

Julie Lasky's *Some People Can't Surf: The Graphic Design of Art Chantry* is a "traditional show-and-tell graphic design book," only with assurance and standing. Chantry's work is original and rich enough to support deep inspection. However, considering its maker, the book's appreciative yet straightforward approach is fitting. Lasky provides illuminating background on the designer and for individual works. Chantry's book design allows that work to speak for itself, and reflects his sensibility. *Some People Can't Surf* is succinct and profound.

The appearance of the "attempted magazine" *Dot Dot Dot* is another encouraging sign that design writing can be eclectic, thoughtful and imaginative. The journal proves there's plenty of unexplored territory for design investigations and the forms they may take. What *Trace* promised, *Dot Dot Dot* provides. The question is if the magazine can find the audience it deserves.

WE MAY BE AT A STAGE when all formal innovations have been exhausted: post-modern postscript time. There is no dominating formality or ideology to produce design. A congeries of theories and practices transcends physical borders. This leaves us with the final and central concerns of making design better, which are extra-design.

For the majority of designers, their activity is a job, a service. To change how they do design, you must change the conditions under which they work. A renovation of capitalism and consumer society is not on graphic design's agenda.

Debate briefly engaged around the "First Things First" manifesto. The turbulence provoked by the statement demonstrates that actual questions were asked. The manifesto was confined somewhat by being a "top down" action; however, it's incontestable that the signatories could exploit their talents to greater profit. And *Adbusters'* addition of a web page where anyone could sign on brought it to the trenches.

The swift passing of the topic is its most disquieting aspect. For many, to raise it at all was an annoyance. Outright dismissals of the manifesto as naïve, elitist, or (at best) impracticable were unsurprising. When you're gaming the system, there's little incentive to change the rules. A startling cynicism was often exhibited under the guise of critical limpidity or pragmatic sobriety. It sadly dovetails with the broader societal conviction that idealism is for chumps.

Every assertion should undergo critical scrutiny. But responsibility accompanies dissension: the duty to advance discussion and promote increasing dialogue. Only if you've announced your support of the *status quo*—and a disinterest in the lot of the less fortunate—do you get to hit and run. Directing a discussion is seemly, squelching it isn't.

It's possible I'm expecting too much too soon of design. Or of people who make it (and make it making it). The channels of commercial determinism are deeply cut. Redirection requires either a massive exertion of force or constant erosion over years. We didn't get here overnight. A major obstacle is an acceptance that the world we have was inevitable. In fact, it was the result of numerous individual actions, from multiple motivations. Each must be traced and assessed.

The change of garde in design has been recent; folks are barely getting settled in. And there aren't many of them. Add to this the fact that you can't control how people interpret what happened. In design, the surface is all that counts.

Design could be a significant agora of discourse, more so than art or other creative disciplines. It's situated closest to the intersection of culture and commerce, the individual and society. What seems at first unwieldy—trying to forge a criticism to reconcile, let's say, the *Catfish* DVD and a bus schedule (or an annual report or a brochure or any familiar artifact) is design's potential. Sometimes it's realized, and it's a revelation to the eye's mind.

The friction between personal investigation such as *Catfish* and public practice (e.g. information graphics) alone is daunting. Positions are frequently staked in one or the other camp and pursued as ends in themselves. Rather than endpoints on an axis, they act across a field of activity that is design. A considered contemplation of how they inform, inspire, and rely on each other is required.

The ultimate disappointment today is that a campaign for critical thinking must again be mounted. We might remember an admonition of Socrates, "The unexamined life is not worth living." An unexamined design isn't worth doing, or seeing.

In the quiet, strange things happen. We think we hear endless, thunderous applause, and steadfastly congratulate ourselves. Breaking the silence could make us realize we're hearing only the roaring of blood in our ears.

Kenneth FitzGerald is an Assistant Professor of Art at Old Dominion University in Norfolk, Virginia; collator of the travelling design exhibition *Adversary*; and agent of *The News of the Whirled*, slated for its fourth and final issue in spring 2003.

Towards Critical Autonomy
or
Can Graphic Design Save Itself?

By Andrew Blauvelt

"ART EXISTS TODAY in a state of pluralism: no style or even mode of art is dominant and no critical position is orthodox. Yet this state is also a position, and this position is an alibi. As a general condition pluralism tends to absorb argument —which is not to say that it does not promote antagonism of all sorts. One can only begin out of a discontent with this *status quo*: for in a pluralist state art and criticism tend to be dispersed and so rendered impotent. Minor deviation is allowed only in order to resist radical change."

Hal Foster, *The Problem with Pluralism*, 1982

IT WOULD BE AN UNDERSTATEMENT to say that the 1990s were an important decade for graphic design. Not only were the technological transformations of the desktop publishing and personal computing revolution of the 1980s fully absorbed, but so, too, were the lessons of formal experimentation that had developed in the academies and the marketplace.

Today, we can reflect fondly on those impassioned debates in the nineties about the merits of computer-aided design and the limits of readability and legibility, or the naiveté of whether we needed only ten typefaces, or the unbridled enthusiasm of the Internet. These issues and many others formed the basis for much design discourse in the first half of the nineties, producing a new generation of voices debating the merits of these changes—many of them in the pages of *Emigre*, myself included.

Slowly the debates subsided. Any tension that may have existed among the factions eased and the marketplace and academy embraced the eclecticism of difference. The globally interconnected and highly disseminated design scene, which really came into the fore in the nineties, could now transplant even the most provincial tendencies in a matter of months. Dabbling in the vernacular "imagescape" of contemporary Los Angeles used to seem like a case of what Kenneth Frampton called "critical regionalism," but now one can find this strategy on view in such far-flung places as Zurich or Bangkok.

Hal Foster's commentary (see epigraph) about the pluralism of the eighties art scene could be easily applied to contemporary graphic design. Significant aesthetic debates have been superseded by consensus; not a fight over which style but agreement on all styles. The fundamental principal of pluralism asks not in what style we should design, but rather that we design stylishly. A plethora of these benign styles exist to mix or match according to the logic of the marketplace. Once style was a defining gesture, unapologetically ideological, and a signal that differentiated and codified its subject. Today style has been reduced to a choice, not a matter of conviction but one of convenience.

This leveling process has also transformed the few avenues and forums for graphic design. Professional organizations, publications, schools, and even competitions used to be distinct. If they are not now defunct, they are pretty much interchangeable. Graduate programs, whether celebrated or scorned, which were once seen as the source of "the problem," now dutifully reproduce their progeny.

This situation of academic and marketplace pluralism, as well as a dearth of critical discourse, are actually related phenomena, each reflecting the condition of the other. Slowly but surely, any critical edge to design—either real or imagined—has largely disappeared, dulled by neglect in the go-go nineties or deemed expendable in the subsequent downswing. However, the reason seems not a factor of cyclical economies, but rather the transfiguration of a critical avant-garde into a post-critical arrière-garde.

It is no wonder that graphic design today feels like a vast formless body able to absorb any blows delivered to it, lacking coherency and increasingly dispersed. This absence of a critical mass or resistant body is at the heart of the current malaise.

One might argue that graphic design today no longer exists in the form, or material body, we once knew it. So scattered and destabilized are its constituent elements that any attempt at definitions becomes meaningless. The expansion of graphic design beyond its roots in print is simply one symptom of this crisis. Even a broad moniker such as "communication design" looses cohesion in the face of a multitude of providers producing all sorts of "communications" for divergent media; be it print, television, video, film, or the Internet. Lacking the specificity of a medium, graphic design tends to be identified more through its varied products than any sense of disciplinary practice. Thus graphic design is reduced to its commodity form–simply a choice of vehicles for delivering a message: ad, billboard, book, brochure, typeface, Web site, and so on. Implicit in this reductive understanding is the denial of graphic design as a disciplinary practice and with it the possibility of disciplinary autonomy.

THE LATE EIGHTIES AND EARLY NINETIES produced an assault on the conventions of graphic design through an intense period of formal experimentation. Those inquiries were a desire to rethink prevailing assumptions, principally the legacy of modernism, which succeeded in breaking the link between modernism and the avant-garde. Up to that point, from the late nineteenth century on, an avant-garde in design existed within the rubric of modernism. Indeed, those experiments in the late eighties and early nineties demonstrated that it was possible to produce a design avant-garde independent of modernism.

But just like the modernist avant-gardes that preceded them, the recent experiments were premised on the notion of inventing new formal languages without historical precedent, or re-presenting historical styles and motifs as pastiche. Paradoxically, much of the theoretical discourse that formed the basis of these experiments espoused a philosophy that dispensed with such notions as originality altogether. Nevertheless, these experiments soon conflated the avant-garde with individual expression (the ultimate "origin" of the designer), as if guarding against the looming specter of anonymity found in the figure of the desk-top publisher. Today, we have become so invested, both profession-ally and educationally, in the quest for new formal languages that the subsequent pluralism that it has wrought goes essentially unchallenged.

The results of most 80s/90s formal experimentation moved quickly from polemic to profitability. Both within the market-place and the academy the consequence was not to invent wholly new languages but rather develop variations of existing styles. The critical reflexivity that had been the genesis of such exper-imental work was pushed aside as the promotion of individual expression became paramount. It is no coincidence that the pro-liferation of design styles corresponded with the increase of the number of brands and the demand for product segmentation in the marketplace. The academy reacted with similar mis-recognition by seeing formal experimentation as an end in itself; whereby the exercise of individual expression (more common-ly called "personal style") was considered experimental. The situation created successive generations of work that had all the look and feel of the experimental without actually being exper-imental. This should be contrasted with the possibility of experimentation that is itself contextual—tied to the continu-ity of a historical discourse of design, for example, one that questions not so much the form of design but the possibilities of its practice.

We need to imagine a historical language of design that tran-scends styles and is embedded in the continuity of discourse. This requires more than what currently passes for graphic design history—a tiresome parade of images devoid of analysis and pack-aged like seasonal trends from Pottery Barn. The present-tense nature of the 90s all but erased historical memory, leaving stu-dents and practitioners unable to chart a course for tomorrow —like a person without a past who has no identity and therefore no future.

One of the more interesting, albeit rare, examples of historical work, is the publication *The World Must Change: Graphic Design and Idealism* published in the Netherlands in 1999. The fact that it is not constructed as a history accounts for part of its allure. Cross-generational in its perspectives, the work considers the role of idealism as it plays out in Dutch design, from the trajectory of early modernist utopian projects, through the increasing rationalization of design in the 1960s and 1970s, to more recent developments that contest the viability of such notions. The authors explore a concept over time drawing connections among different generations of designers. Such an approach gets beneath the various period styles and formal affectations resplendent in Dutch design to explore a perceived tendency within the practice in a varied way, from the historical to the theoretical to the personal.

AN IMPORTANT WAY OUT of the conditions of a commensurate pluralism is for graphic design to reclaim a position of critical autonomy. By autonomy, I do not mean a wholesale withdrawal from the social or the kind of freedoms the fine arts claim. Graphic design, precisely because it is an instrumental form of communication, cannot divorce itself from the world. Rather, graphic design must be seen as a discipline capable of generating meaning on its own terms without undue reliance on commissions, prescriptive social functions, or specific media or styles. Such actions should demonstrate self-awareness and self-reflexivity; a capacity to manipulate the system of design for ends other than those imposed on the field from without, and to question those conventions formed from within.

A newly engaged form of critical practice is necessary, one that is no longer concerned with originality as defined by personal expression, but rather one dedicated to an inventive contextuality. Uniqueness should be located in the myriad circumstances and plethora of social and cultural contexts in which design finds itself. Too much time and energy is devoted to the object culture of graphic design, its production and processes, and too little on its effects. We need more why and less how, as the late Tibor Kalman once remarked.

So, what is critical design? I'll resort to a definition provided by Anthony Dunne and Fiona Raby who, conveniently, teach in the Critical Design Unit at the Royal College of Art in London. Dunne and Raby teach and practice product design outside the norm, constructing an alternative vision through projects which utilize design objects they create in order to probe the conditions and social effects of electronic products on our culture. Dunne and Raby explain:

"[Critical Design] differs from experimental design, which seeks to extend the medium, extending it in the name of progress and aesthetic novelty. Critical design takes as its medium social, psychological, cultural, technical, and economic values, in an effort to push the limits of lived experience not the medium."
Design Noir, 2001.

While Dunne and Raby work within, alongside and against the field of product design, their notion of critical design could easily apply to graphic design. Critical design is non-affirming, that is to say, it refuses or at least is skeptical of the conventional role of design as a service provider to industry. Critical design is polemical, it asks questions and poses problems for the profession and users alike, it is opposed to traditional notions of problem-solving, and it eschews the singularity of a medium in favor of the multiplicities of social agency and effects.

The point is not to invent a neo-modernist avant-garde and

all of its inherent problems. Rather, the purpose is to stake a claim for autonomy, which, like an avant-garde, is already a separation from the social demands that limit graphic design to its most marketable features. Autonomy also gives coherency to graphic design in order to resist the dispersal it currently suffers by defining the conditions and terms under which it seeks to operate. Most importantly, a space of autonomy for graphic design affords an opportunity to engage in a more critical examination of its practice, assuming that it does not lapse into a convenient formalism or cannot escape the ideology of expressionism.

Andrew Blauvelt is the Design Director at the Walker Art Center in Minneapolis.

Visitations

BY Denise Gonzales Crisp
Kali Nikitas & Louise Sandhaus

Following are excerpts from a series of online chats that took place in September 2002 between Louise Sandhaus in California, Kali Nikitas in Minnesota and Denise Gonzales Crisp in North Carolina. Together, these three designers/educators had taken a two-week trip in June to Holland and London to visit designers and design schools, museums and fashion houses. These chats reflect on the state of graphic design as they encountered it, and were also meant to help inspire and inform the three as they returned to teaching and developing their curricula at California Institute of the Arts, Minneapolis College of Art and Design, and NCSU's College of Design, respectively.

DENISE: What motivated you two to organize this trip?

KALI: As the chair of a graphic design program, it was important to reacquaint myself with the European design community, both for my own growth and to set up potential relationships with studios and schools for study abroad, internships, visiting artists, etc.

LOUISE: I work with an astounding faculty, but I still felt I needed to expand my scope of influence and be exposed to the ideas and issues that designers in other countries are dealing with.

KALI: I was reminded how a different political and social climate affects designers and their work philosophy and formal expression. I noticed a lot of simple, clean work and

the need to make design be more than just pretty,
particularly in the exhibition we saw at the Design
Museum in London, curated by Emily King and Christian
Küsters.

LOUISE: I wrote a review of that show for *Eye*. It was based on
the book *Restart*, which was about the response by
designers to an exhausted postmodern chaos through
creative use of systems or sets of rules to define the
process...

DENISE: ...that can also control the outcome of the form. My
sense is that design studios, and education programs –
or maybe the more progressive design programs – are
starting to ask how designers might contribute more
deeply to the process of design. How they can find
themselves both at the core of developing systems that
continue to generate form, as well as making the end
product, and understanding how these forms work in the
culture.

LOUISE: Yes, but in some of these programs it seems that the
more designers get involved in the "product," the more
the development of the visual form as a significant contribution to the function of the work gets diminished or
overwhelmed.

KALI: Which is a big mistake.

DENISE: Right. Can you say Jakob Nielsen?

KALI: When you believe that form is not important, you are
being naïve or lazy.

DENISE: What about the form we encountered in Holland and
England? Are the designers we talked to developing
systems at the expense of the form?

KALI: Depends on the designer. Take Foundation 33. They stick
to systems so much that the form does not vary much from
project to project. The form suffers. Experimental Jet Set,

Graphic Thought Facility (and the list goes on, including designers in the U.S.), have made some interesting systems that have generated some interesting forms, but by now they're a bit trendy and predictable.

DENISE: Would you say Experimental Jet Set was among the originators of this trend, though? I ask, because I do think some of their work is attempting to find intelligent responses to style-mongering. Unfortunately, the forms their systems generate are borrowed from the "unemotive" universal-minded sixties.

LOUISE: Some of their work reminds me of 60s conceptualism, of Sol Lewitt's manifesto. Lewitt said that "Banal ideas cannot be rescued by beautiful form."

KALI: I'm thinking about the *Conceptual Art* show we saw at the Stedelijk Museum in Amsterdam. The work in that exhibition was beautiful and rooted in new ways of thinking. The form that those artists created was not boring, maybe because the form was a natural expression of the times.

DENISE: It's no accident that this show was curated now. Clearly there's a trend toward, or back to, a type of conceptualism filled with thick and juicy ideas. Graphic designers seem to have adopted the look, too, though. Which is why I think the trend toward sixties and seventies Modernism is as much about mining the past (pomo) as it is an attempt to redirect our values.

LOUISE: I wonder if 60s-style conceptualism really ever went away in Europe. I'd also like to point out that there are two kinds of conceptualism. There's the conceptualism that tries to get the material object out of the equation. For instance, *Shoot*, the 1971 performance by artist Chris Burden, where he had someone shoot him in the arm, was about an experience as a work of art rather than as an object. Then there's the conceptualism in which the system *is* the idea, which finds its expression in a particular visual form.

DENISE: I'm thinking of Karl Gerstner and his modular systems, which generated and regenerated form like a machine, and new form at that. This isn't what we saw in Europe, though.

KALI: No, it's not. We saw designers who were either ignoring history, or were unaware of history.

DENISE: Right. Remember, Experimental Jet Set even said that in Europe, Helvetica is just a typeface, and doesn't mean what it might in the U.S. I guess that does indicate they're aware, though.

LOUISE: From what I could tell, very little history, design or otherwise, is taught in the schools we visited. "Now" seems to be a blank slate that arrived from nowhere.

KALI: And look at how few of the designers we visited were interested in what we are doing or what is happening in the U.S.

DENISE: Did anyone ever ask about our work, our programs?

KALI: That's my question. Maybe my expectations of the profession are too high. Since school, I have been interested in what is happening on both coasts as well as across the ocean. I think everyone should look beyond their backyard. It seems natural to have a dialogue with designers in other countries. But maybe our education was unique. And maybe the Europeans we met are content and aren't looking elsewhere for any answers.

LOUISE: I also want to bring up Hal Foster's new book *Design and Crime*, which is a melancholic reflection on design. He talks about Rem Koolhaas — an architect who generates unique, well-researched descriptions of contemporary cultural conditions into which his designs are supposed to function. For instance, the project on China and the one on shopping that he did with the Harvard students, where they create over-the-top, comprehensive, doorstopper compendiums of the history and circumstances of an existing cultural situation. Rather than imagining utopian or idealized conditions, he and the students are more interested in describing a condition that actually exists. I'm guessing he does this to get a better grasp of what to design before considering what the designed thing looks like. But there doesn't seem to be a consideration of the social or political agendas that these situations that he's describing represent. And so there's no response in the design solution to that part of reality, including the possibility of saying "This isn't the future I want to live in," and perhaps offering some viable, alternative proposal. Some of the graphic design work we saw had a similarly partially blind agenda. And unlike Rem's projects, there seems to be little knowledge of the past, no vision of the future, no reason why anything is being made.

DENISE: This lack of a greater context is the true issue for me. And as you suggest, it is what seemed to have gone missing in what we saw in Europe. So many designers were attempting to find something meaningful. And I applaud that. Yet the result still seemed to end up being capital "D" design. For me, much of what we saw still comes back to a wholesale acceptance of what graphic design is supposed to look like. No one we visited, except maybe Goodwill and Graphic Thought Facility, was attempting to challenge D-esign.

LOUISE: Design vs. design?

DENISE: Big D design is where the only goal is to create appropriate solutions to any so-called problem provided by a client, where the drive toward resolution overwhelms exploration of other formal possibilities. This kind of work must always look like design, rather than, by contrast, looking like, well, design informed by things other than graphic design!

LOUISE: Let's follow through on the Goodwill example. He struck a chord.

DENISE: Yes, I think he touched a major nerve.

KALI: My first reaction to his work was "how familiar!" The thinking and form — it looked like CalArts work from the late 80s.

LOUISE: I think the work was incredibly nihilistic. It depressed me. The idea that even common sense or thoughtfulness could be abandoned and the work could still be considered design.

DENISE: For me, Goodwill was one of the few designers attempting to break away from the dictates of Euro-determined design. Anti-style (and I agree, been-there-done-that), but also anti-Modern. And that's another step in the right direction as far as I'm concerned.

LOUISE: But his work gives up hope that design — not as a mere exercise in aesthetics, but as shaping of thought and thoughtful shaping — has significance. I can appreciate what you're saying, Denise. And yes, over-aesthetisized work is tiresome. But works intended as public communications done without intention to further that function?! Sorry, but it's really a sign of "why bother, it's all crap and doesn't matter anyway" to me. Excuse me while I get a handkerchief, sniff, sniff.

DENISE: Shaping significance is most closely tied today to shaping systems. And this is among the things Goodwill was attempting, whether he knew it or not. He is shaping systems that don't manifest as groovy computer form, that aren't modular and "high level" views, but systems that might move us past taste or personal expression as a guiding principle, and into forms that reflect and interact with users, clients, designers, everybody.

LOUISE: So Denise, your answer is "don't shape at all"?!

DENISE: No. But think of the way an imprinted address on a
piece of direct mail interferes with tidy æsthetics. He's just
corralling some of that. At least he wasn't quoting high-
Modern design as if it were so much vernacular.

LOUISE: But he was using vernacular; the vernacular of default!

KALI: Louise, you mean that "default" equals not originating or
designing the form? And that he seems to be assuming,
because he is being conceptual, that the form he creates
will automatically be meaningful?

LOUISE: Yes. Actually, it's something I'd say was pervasive in
much of the work we saw elsewhere. I call it the "style of the
everyday." And it reflects what I believe is the continuing
crisis of representation; that is, the problem that designers
like Goodwill have with representing a world that is so full
of complexity, information, and contradictions that no one
feels up to the challenge of representing it. Instead, we get
non-representation. Defaults. They leave everything "as is."

KALI: I have a different take on him. I perceive Goodwill as
trying to distinguish himself by exploring issues such as
designer-as-author, or designer-as-director-of-audience-
experience. And he is struggling with it. He should have
been in contact with American designers, because these
issues were explored in the late 80s and 90s at schools like
Cranbrook, CalArts, and Yale. He could have saved himself
a lot of time if he had been exposed to these explorations.

DENISE: Still, his method is at least one way to get design
practice to reflect more depth, to represent actual living
beings instead of Martha-matons. This is the concern I
continue to see surfacing over and over, in Europe, and the
U.S. Goodwill seems to be trying to make things meaningful
by disregarding or kicking at design Euro-standards. And I

agree with this push. Though, as Kali said, maybe it's what we saw going on in the U.S. a while ago.

DENISE: Let's talk about what we might be carrying around as a sort of souvenir from this trip, something we refer to in our thoughts, a teeny muse.

LOUISE: I saw a textile design at Central St. Martins and RCA. The stuff was so compelling. It was conceptually based and so full of energy and visceral. By comparison, the graphic design work we saw looked limp.

KALI: I remember the dinner with Rick Vermeulen, and the chef who promised us a great meal and delivered! And Rick's work, which still resonates with me.

DENISE: His is the one poster I put up upon returning. Very vital stuff, still, for me too.

LOUISE: There were the Leopold and Rudolf Blaschka glass sea creatures at the Design Museum in London. Their radiance outshined the *Graphics Now* show in the next room.

LOUISE: And Karel Marten's grand-baby announcement.

DENISE: And the layers of history and decoration in the streets of Amsterdam. The work you mention bore out passionate responses to making. Maybe as designers, we all just want to move beyond the overly designed object, or that oh-so-clever graphic aloofness. These things we are reacting to have what in common?

LOUISE: Passion, yes. Caring. The sign that something matters!

DENISE: I'm afraid I found so much joy in non-design things that it seems immaterial to our conversation. In Antwerp, the view out my window of the wrought iron pensione sign set against the massive carved stone tower of the cathedral. Or not understanding a politically charged argument over architecture, in Dutch, during a lecture at the back of a restaurant in Amsterdam with Henk Elenga occasionally translating in my ear. Or the intense red and green where that working-class strip mall was converted into a living lesson in art.

LOUISE: We're bad. No wonder so many cringe at calling themselves graphic designers. Even we champions of graphic design found so much more outside design to move us.

DENISE: Don't you think we're in a unique position as Americans to play many sides at once?

LOUISE: We *are* in a unique position to ask "what do we want to invent for this culture?"

DENISE: Right, we need to create rather than react.

KALI: This trip reminded me that when one is a full-time designer, there is little room for questioning, challenging, and shifting the profession. As teachers, we're in a privileged position to effect change with our students, and maybe also take risks in our own practice.

LOUISE: We have *got* to get over the *Adbusters* mentality in academia. Instead of critiquing everything and complaining, we have the opportunity to really address our society and culture. But we must have some sort of picture about our hopes and dreams for the culture and the society in which we live, and then build something that will further that vision. But I want to emphasize the need to accept this culture as it is, and take ideas from and insert ideas into that culture.

DENISE: While I agree that the *Adbusters* approach isn't as productive as social service, for instance, it does inform about issues otherwise left unaddressed.

KALI: But it tends to ignore complexity. We can challenge and should challenge, yes. But please, let's look at the bigger picture.

Design Modernism 8.0

By Mr. Keedy

"Everything has been done!" is the reason often cited for the lack of excitement in design lately. It is true. On a superficial level, every new digital gimmick has been done and most of the "rules" have been broken a few times. But just because someone has planted their flag on the tip of the iceberg and moved on, this hardly means there is nothing left to explore. Only the most obvious moves and gestures have been made in our still new digital world. Who cares who made them?

I made a few of them myself, and I remember the panic it created in the late 80s and early 90s when a few designers were experimenting with Postmodern ideas. They were called "ugly" and "chaos" and "design for designers" (whatever that means). The call to return to Modernism started almost immediately, even though hardly anyone had actually abandoned it. Since those "ugly" days, designers have felt compelled to update and reaffirm Modernism, so graphic design won't have to submit itself to the Postmodern complications that most other cultural practices struggle with. Also, for a lot of graphic designers, Modernism can never end because without its easy set of grids, rules, and systems, they would be clueless.

Ironically, each successive version of Modernism seems to include more ideas from Postmodernism. The first was Dan Friedman's "Radical Modernism"[1] of 1994, which called for a kinder, gentler Modernism. Then Andrew Blauvelt's "Complex Simplicity"[2] contrasted the excessively complex (but stale) work of the 90s with the simple (yet memorable) modernism of the new millennium. One of the latest European incarnations of Modernism can be found in *Restart: New Systems in Graphic Design*,[3] in which we learn:

> "What at the outset had seemed a critical challenge to the rigid mindset of Modernism had degenerated into a visual free-for-all. Design commentators began to notice a move away from the 'Postmodern style' as early as 1995, when Dutch critic Carel Kuitenbrouwer wrote of a 'new sobriety' in Dutch graphic design. Turning their back on free expression, graphic designers opted for restraint — and this is where the system comes in."

Here we have all the main themes in the popular version of recent events in graphic design; Modernism was briefly disrupted by a "Postmodern style" that started as "critical challenge" but quickly "degenerated into a visual free-for-all" only to be rejected for a retooled version of Modernism complete with "new" systems. All of which sounds much better than saying that graphic designers, when faced with the "critical challenge" of Postmodernism, only understood its most "degenerate" forms and failed to comprehend, much less accept, the challenges and opportunities it presented. Instead, graphic designers retreated into a less rigorous version of Modernism, a style I call "Modernism 8.0" (the latest upgrade since the first release over eighty years ago).

The most recent salvos in the fight to keep modernism alive in the hearts and minds of graphic designers are coming from *Dot Dot Dot* magazine.[4] This design magazine (or "attempt" at a design magazine, according to its editors) is not as critical of designers as it is of the idea of design itself. But in spite of all its earnest hand-wringing about the glossy paper, white space, decorative layouts, and portfolio presentations of other design magazines, and the pious vow to be critical, rigorous, and useful, it is still primarily another style bible for yet another style: Modernism 8.0.

Most design magazines are about form as content. But *Dot Dot Dot* is about content as form. The problem, of course, is that content doesn't have an implicit form, because form is realized only through individual/personal perception and conception. But Modernism's true believers think they can present content with only a minimal interference from style, an idea that is based largely on personal bias, but is being held up as truth or reality. There is a word for people who believe in universal truths in spite of overwhelming contradictory evidence: they're called Fundamentalist.

The problem that Modernists have with style is that sooner or later everything goes out of style because formal preference is too subjective. Eventually all forms and styles will be seen as deficient or problematic. Your taste will always reveal your weakness. Therefore, it takes a bit of courage to go out on a limb with style. It's a chance many designers are simply not willing to take anymore. Why? The styles and forms that are considered "classics" have achieved their lofty status simply by being the least embarrassing. Are designers really so mortified that their old work, at some point in the future, will look out-of-step and too revealingly individual rather than timeless and universal?

Modernism 8.0 adopts a style-phobic attitude to form-making and a back-to-basics theory of pseudo-scientific faith in objectivity, incongruously teamed up with an "anything goes" relativism resurrected (like bellbottoms) from the 60s and 70s. Never mind that it was a spectacular failure the first time around. In a few cases I suspect the appeal of relativist functionalism is to be cynically subversive. But in most cases it is just a naive, self-censoring, limited vocabulary of forms and concepts that lacks the sophistication to comprehend, much less speak about, its own impoverishment.

Utility is the bottom line in graphic design. It's what makes something "design" and not art or religion. But the designation of utility as some kind of golden rule or criterion for evaluation doesn't work. Blind faith in the objectivity of the designer's conception of function is unsupportable without subjective qualifiers. The myth of objectivity and faith in abstraction are cultural constructs that designers use to perpetuate an illusion of consensus and certainty, recasting personal bias (style) as universally accepted principles.

Modernism 8.0 truly offers the worst of both worlds. From Modernism it takes systems, reductivism, and a dogmatic style, and from Postmodernism it takes relativism, low vernacular taste, and pedantic self-indulgence. Creating "systems" that can be used as both a crutch and shield, it is neither ambitious nor inspiring, aiming low to successfully meet its goal. Encouraged by the juvenile world of pop culture, the short-sighted ambition to be new, cool, and transgressive has only led to conformity, with designers passively following instead of challenging each other.

Modernism 8.0 is most popular with anyone who wants to look cool without appearing self-conscious or opinion-ated and who suspects that design is by its very nature inauthentic. They do not want things to look "designed," because they think they will look "fake." This assertion is true only if you happen to be an imbecile. Most of us are complex beings with needy minds that can't stop scrutinizing our environment for patterns of meaning to assimilate into useful knowledge. That is our nature. And graphic design, through specific, personal gestures, addresses this need.

Conversely, the myth of authentic, undesigned communication is a fantasy — a nostalgia for a primal state that resides somewhere outside of human experience. Like all myths, its function is to help people cope with the paradoxical nature of existence by providing simple answers. But design is too pervasive and elusive. You can't satisfactorily define it in simple terms, nor can you ever reject it.

CUTEISM

Cuteism is the vernacular style that Modernism 8.0 uses to soften its hard edges and warm up its frigid disposition. Like a pink terry-cloth slipcover on a Breuer chair, it makes everything warm and fuzzy. However, the sugar and spice of Cuteism is more than just candy sprinkles on a modernist cake. Cuteism is really about empowerment. Toddlers are the prototype for the whole cute aesthetic; we associate their vulnerability with our own sense of empowerment and entitlement. That is why cute things give us a happy and reassuring feeling that works even when we know the trick. The pathetic weakness of others makes us feel powerful enough to be empathetic and proud of our own benevolence. Cute, huh?

In a world that is often ugly and unsympathetic there is nothing wrong with making cute or frivolous things. But a little bit of it goes a long way — at least for grown-ups. At the start of the digital revolution, I remember thinking that graphic designers would soon be authoring nonlinear interactive hypertextual narratives that incorporate text, sound, and motion into a new paradigm for communication.

But all we got was a bunch of silly cartoons.

It may be the influence of the computer, but it is certainly not the computer's fault that so many designers have limited themselves to a basic vocabulary of geometric form (the Infantile Style), and are inarticulate in the visual languages of ornament and decoration. Most designers today can't tell the difference between Greek, Chinese or Celtic motifs, much less invent a contemporary decorative style. Instead, we get the crude collages of bad little boys, and the puffy fluff of cute little girls — the complicit vernacular of Modernism 8.0.

I think Owen Jones said it best in his 1856 design classic, *The Grammar of Ornament* [5] :

> "All compositions of squares or circles will be monotonous, and afford but little pleasure, because the means whereby they are produced are very apparent. So we think that compositions distributed in equal lines or divisions will be less beautiful than those which require a higher mental effort to appreciate them . . . we shall find it to be universally the case, that in the best periods of art all moldings and ornaments were founded on curves of the higher order, such as the conic sections; whilst, when art declined circles and compass work were much more dominant."

Working with a reductive palette of forms doesn't nec-essarily have to lead to the decline of Western civilization. But in combination with reductive concepts and minimal skills, it might. If you look back at the work of designers and illustrators who worked with a reductive palette, like the Beggerstaff Brothers, Aubrey Beardsly, and E. Knight McCauffer (to name a few), it is difficult to deny that their work has an emotional depth and formal complexity well beyond anything you see in our age of technological superiority. Although they worked in a simple manner, the ideas and emotions they were expressing were not simplistic. They used geometric construction and a reduced color palette as a means, not an end, in expressing their ideas. Now it seems the means are the ends, and the concept is the form. What you see is what you get, and what you get isn't much. Sometimes being cute just isn't enough, and when you think about it, it's not even very nice.

IN-*FAUX*-MATION GRAPHICS

Displaying the contents page on the cover of a book in imitation of academic journals, reproducing full pages as miniature thumb nails as in instructional diagrams, and regurgitating mass quantities of fake information or raw useless data in an interesting but ultimately arbitrary fashion, are a few of the favorite gimmicks used to demonstrate that design is about ideas and not just style.

Modernism 8.0's reductivist, functionalist faith in objectivity, and ambition to be newer (but less rigorous) than the old functionalism, has led to a pseudo-intellectual approach I call "In-*faux*-mation Graphics." The look is serious and informative, and aesthetic pleasure is supposed to be found in the organization of information rather than its formal presentation. The fact that the "systems" don't make sense, or in any way aid the reader's comprehension, is apparently a minor detail. Like the worst of the early Postmodern experiments, it looks smart and seems to mean something. But instead of the surprise of meaning all you get is a feeling of exasperation.

It should come as no surprise that in our saturated information age, information itself, or more specifically, raw data, would be fetishized.[6] Designers tend to use the words "data" and "information" interchangeably. In fact, they rarely use the word "data" at all, as if data automatically becomes information in their hands. For many designers, data signifies ideas and thinking. It is prominently displayed as proof of their conceptual practice. The idea that design is about ideas and thinking is a well-worn cliché. But how true is it? To non-designers it only sounds like hubris, as if graphic designers cornered the intellectual market with their visual puns and "big ideas" that operate on the conceptual level of knock-knock jokes.

By avoiding style as much as possible, and by refusing to express a point of view, the in-*faux*-mation designer turns their audience into a search engine responsible for generating the meaning that the designer was too afraid or too lazy to provide. Anyone with the ability, or more importantly, the patience, to decipher these gratuitous data dumps is rewarded with the realization that they just wasted their time.

The unique expertise of graphic designers is to make visual communication a memorable and enriching experience. It is exactly this act of creativity that is the "baby" that some designers are throwing out with the "bathwater" of style, just so they can be fashionable and show how darned conceptual they are. That is also why looking at their work is like staring at an empty tub. There is no point in critiquing the design decisions the designer made, because they didn't really make any. As a strategy, it is an end-game move towards design without designers.

DESIGNERLESS DESIGN; THE LAST BIG THING

The historically-challenged designers who think that everything has been done, and who see style as only a byproduct of problem-solving and who subscribe to other such Modernist claptrap, have found the ultimate solution to the style problem. The latest and last new thing left to do: nothing. But since it is impossible to literally do nothing, one must develop systems, and construct (design?) the illusion of doing nothing. The style of no style has to look designerless. No self to express, no showy demonstration of technical craft or expertise. Just let the software do the designing. No new or fashionable fonts, no obscure, nostalgic, or historical fonts. Just generic snapshots, artless diagrams, and Helvetica on a grid. It is phony functionalism that tries to make a virtue out of poverty, turning the crystal goblet into a styrofoam cup.

One might be willing to accept the Modernist conceit that there is an intrinsic beauty in simplicity (an idea stolen from the East). But elevating banality and nothing as a new and interesting alternative to the spectacle of something is just dumb. This is Modernism that has gone sour because it's way past its expiration date. Ironically, it takes restraint, attention to detail, and a lack of ego (sounds like a Modernist mantra), for a college-educated professional designer to pull this style off. Amateurs however, can accomplish it effortlessly.

Dot Dot Dot magazine almost looks, at first glance, like a zine by someone who has no particular interest in graphic design. Closer inspection, however, reveals a fussy designerly touch behind the affected styleless style. Indifference is too hard to fake. Although I find this designerless design style interesting, and I appreciate the practitioner's ingenuity and ambition to keep pressing forward in the good ol' Modernist avant-garde tradition, I have to wonder where it will take them, or us, graphic designers. If it's the ideas and social/political issues that really matter, and stylistic and formal communication is of little consequence, then what do we need designers for? Critical thinking and organizing data visually into useful information is something most educated people can master. And to have ideas or a social and political agenda is certainly not something unique to graphic designers. To further their own agendas, graphic designers have successfully held hostage the means of production of visual communication. But the liberation of the means of production is imminent, and graphic designers will have to make a convincing case for themselves to justify their existence.

If designers have a place as specialized cultural workers in the twenty-first century, I doubt if it will be as Modernist drones continuing the Modernist project. That task will be automated, carried out by early digital technologies and late global capitalism. I think it's safe to say that consumerism and pop culture have embraced Modernism, and no longer need designers to keep the faith.

Modernism may be good enough for corporate branding, globalism, and cultural institutions, but it is pretty crappy for people. It doesn't address the complex messiness of real lives lived by real people, and it rejects much of our cultural heritage and diversity. Its obsessive preoccupation with newness for its own sake becomes increasingly dangerous as our technologies become increasingly powerful. Instead of willfully ignoring the failure of Modernism, graphic designers should have faced their Postmodern reality with critical optimism, not cynical detachment.

As the early Modernists predicted, art has gone into life, into our everyday world, and now the real action is in design. It's just going to take a bit longer for everyone to acknowledge that. But I'm sure they will in this century. The only question is, who will be calling the shots? A few competing ineffectual design organizations? The advertising-driven design press? Insular, pandering, academic institutions? Condescending cultural institutions? Commercially dependent design professionals? Or everyone else?

Mr. Keedy is a designer, writer, type designer, and educator who lives in Los Angeles.

1. *Radical Modernism*, Dan Friedman, Yale University Press, 1994.
2. "Towards A Complex Simplicity," Andrew Blauvelt, *Eye* magazine, No. 35, Vol. 9, Spring 2000.
3. *Restart: new Systems in Graphic Design*, Edited by Christian Küster and Emily King, Thames & Hudson 2001.
4. *Dot Dot Dot* magazine, Broodje & Kaas Publishing, NL, UK, DE, 2000.
5. *The Grammar of Ornament*, Owen Jones, first published in 1856 by Day & Sons, Lincoln's Inn Fields, London. Published in the United States by DK Publishing, inc. 2001.
6. Karim Rashid, the hip industrial designer of the moment, has coined the term "info-thetics," — the æsthetics of information. Although he says it is easier to do two dimensionally, he is trying to do 3D info-thetics design "that can say something about the digital age." *IdN* magazine, No. 2, Vol. 9, 2002.

More on next page

OLD MODERNISM

1   Mostly black & white with primary and a bit of tertiary color

2   Helvetica

3   White space

4   Big ideas, and visual puns everyone understands

5   Organizing principles expressed through rigorously articulated systems

6   Form follows function

7   Iconic

8   Less is more

9   Bars and rule lines

10   Artiness expressed through collages

11   Imitates fine art

12   Geometric abstraction

13   Form is always derived from content

14   Ornament is crime

15   A pure expression of formalist abstraction

16   Precision craftsmanship

17   Simplicity is best

MODERNISM 8.0

1   Mostly black & white with tertiary and a bit of
    primary color
2   Helvetica
3   Empty space
4   Little ideas and visual slapstick nobody understands
5   Organizing principles expressed through vague and
    mutable systems
6   Form follows function, but function is negotiable
7   Banal
8   Less is safe
9   Underlines and strikethroughs
10 Artiness expressed through crude collages
11 Imitates fine art
12 Bitmapped abstraction
13 Form is always provided by software
14 What's an ornament?
15 An obvious repression of any expression
16 Whatever
17 Simplistic is popular

Wonders Revealed:
DESIGN AND *FAUX* SCIENCE

BY JESSICA HELFAND & WILLIAM DRENTTEL

0.001. Real Science

From global warming to genetic cloning to persist-ent threats of bioterrorism, science—perhaps more than any other discipline—is revolutionizing the world. As a cultural influence its reach is pervasive: from stem cell research to sustainable agriculture, it affects what we eat and breathe, where and why and how we behave the way we do. In a very real sense, science is the connective tissue linking past to pres-ent to future, and in this context, its relationship to visual communication is critical. It is through graphic design that the complexities and wonders of science are revealed.

So why are there so few designers participating in the artic-ulation, expression and dissemination of these new ideas? Why isn't there a more central, intellectually relevant and cre-atively meaningful role for designers—one that revolves less around aestheticizing preexisting content and is based, instead, on inventing new ways to visualize these new ideas?

Remarkably, there has been little evidence of any significant response from the design profession, other than the superficial appropriations of the visual language of science that sudden-ly seem to be springing up in every design annual, in every monograph, in every design school critique. Science is the new style idiom of choice, with designers everywhere parroting its visual currencies, adopting its formal vocabularies, stealing its lingo, its acronyms, its cool, cryptic code. But these are cosmetic enhancements, visual conceits which by and large lack a fundamental knowledge of the underlying discipline itself. For design—a profession that once prided itself on translating form into content—such ignorance is alarming, and the false piety is disturbingly disingenuous. Consider the frequency with which periodic tables have recently been graphically revived, harmoniously constructed graphic tropes that invoke the visual language of Mendeleyev's classic grid to codify everything from hardware to cereal to Strathmore's guide to cultural elements. It is as if science offers a kind of credibility that design itself lacks, an instant validation and a seriousness of purpose that, quite possibly, design never had in the first place.

This new seeking after scientific style—let's call it *Faux Science*—is the antithesis of modernism: it's form awaiting content, or worse, serious form retrofitted with interchangeable content. So DNA is used as a paradigm for business strategy; our genetic legacies are reborn as branding schemes for bran flakes. Petrie dishes are procured as objects of desire, inhabited by blurry bacteria used to metaphorically represent everything from bus schedules to bleach advertisements to the end of civilization itself. Designers document and chronicle and organize and record and list and process and craft endless diagrams with carefully plotted line weights and meticulously managed color specs, but what do they really know about enzymes or molecules or the structure of an atom? What do they really know about the world?

Filtered through design's brutally neutralizing style engine, contemporary design is anesthetized and stripped of its indigenous qualities: science, in this context, is a graphic placebo. Meanwhile, designers conceal their intellectual weightlessness and flex their stylistic muscle, producing work that strikes just the right tone of Lab Chic.

And there they stand, positioned ever so meekly at the periphery of this new century, contributing nothing of substance to these, the most critical communication needs of our time.

And designers ask why design doesn't matter.

0.002. *Faux* Science

"Science," wrote Heidegger, "is one of the most essential phenomena of the modern age." It's hygienic and objective, rational and finite, grounded in numerical certainty and cosmological reason. Science is all about clarity and specificity and rationalism, about charting DNA strands and analyzing chemical compounds, about physical density and gravitational pull and a reality that is anything but virtual. And in a world in which design has not only *gone* virtual but, in the process, become overtaken by catastrophically invasive degrees of public interaction, "science" itself has become unusually tantalizing. Gone are the days of thick eyeglasses and plastic pocket protectors, of nerds and slide rules and chemistry sets. In today's anything-goes world of relentless self-expression, science has become the designers' safe haven. It's the new "look and feel."

And it's an easy one to imitate. We grasp its formal conceits —its systematic language of documentation, its methodical alignments—and parlay them into a visual language that resonates with kick-ass authority. It's a safe, if counterfeit, posture for design, redolent of an aesthetic mindset that seems permanently lodged in the visual gestalt of circa-1965 Ciba Geigy pharmaceutical ephemera. Clean and lean. Formulaic. New and improved.

It's the DamienHirstization of everyday life.

0.003. False Authority

The appeal of information design is that it offers instant cred-ibility. This is the domain of numbers and bullets and charts and graphs, ordered lists that visualize the obvious. Information design is rational and authoritative, classified and controlled to within an inch of its life: everything in its place and a place for everything. Label it information design and it looks seri-ous. Number it and it looks scientific.

But it's a false authority, particularly because we buy into the form so unquestioningly. Perhaps this is why so much information design looks alike, ratified by an alarmingly robust strain of Swiss modernism that obliterates the chance for a more expressive design idiom, a more content-driven form. It's also annoyingly ahistorical—unconcerned with earlier sour-ces and ignorant of alternative models that would, arguably, introduce a more original point of view.

Information design has become its own legitimizing force, regardless of its content or context. It's modernism run amok: form *masquerading* as content.

0.004. Panaceas

In biology, the term "morphology" refers to the basic form and structure of organisms without consideration of func-tion. And that is precisely what the morphology (or shape) of elliptical forms seems to be. Yet if the lozenge shapes we see everywhere bear little resemblance to the content they frame or to the function they are intended to illuminate, then what meaning do they have, and what purpose, if any, do they actu-ally serve? Unlike the tangible and quantifiable world of biology, here in the graphical realm such "organisms" are not only function-free, they are little more than ornamental. They're graphic panaceas: a visual cure-all.

Biology, of course, isn't the only discipline in which morphology plays a central role. In the language of numbers, there is *mathematical* morphology, which concentrates on stochastic geometry, random set theory and image algebra. In the lexicon of infertility, there is *reproductive* morphology, in which sperm are analyzed for their morphology, or shape (along with mobility, or speed, and motility, or motion). Finally, in *linguistics*, morphology is the study of the form and structure of words. Here, it can include deviations and inflections, random detours from the essential "shape" of things.

Nevertheless, the preponderance of lozenge shaped *objets* in contemporary graphic matter suggests that it is this very deviation that has perhaps superseded everything else, celebrating form—perhaps even at the expense of content itself.

0.005. Documenting

Combine the urge to collect with the inclination to organize, and the resulting activity offers a unique assortment of scientific pretensions. In documenting, designers dutifully observe the minutiae of their efforts, recording with a detail-consciousness bordering on the absurd.

Not long ago, we attended a graduate design thesis review featuring several months' worth of lint recovered from a clothes dryer. The cumulative, color-coded evidence of this rather bizarre little odyssey in textile hygiene was presented, like a rare archaeological specimen, in an oversized glass vase located—where else?—on eBay.

(Jesse Gordon's portrait, *The Oldest Piece of Dust*, offers a slightly more ironic, though equally detailed study of the design of detritus.*)

This is navel-gazing raised to new and rather worrisome levels: the designer is so busy organizing, it is unlikely that s/he will have time or distance or objectivity to transcend the work through insight, observation, scrutiny, or point of view, any of which might celebrate the power of an original idea. God forbid anyone should have an original idea. We're just too busy documenting it all.

0.006. Cataloguing

Do we strip visual information of its natural scale and emphasis, and in the process, streamline form to negate design's meaning and message? Or do we just make it look good by making it look clean, orderly, cross-referential?

The popularity of the full-bleed photographic tome is based upon an exhaustively micro-managed cataloging of, well, pretty much anything. This inclination to make 300-page books of endless (and often word-free) photographic sequences is science gone astray; for where the scientist analyzes, the designer merely amasses. The poor reader is left to make sense of it all, to locate some hidden narrative or excavate some profound meaning as a consequence of meandering through interminable juxtapositions of intentionally non-linear thinking: so Times Square (turn the page) becomes Beijing (turn the page) becomes a little girl's hand poetically situated against a cloud (turn the page) becomes a wad of colorless chewing gum stuck to the bottom of a chair. Full-bleed image saturation abounds: it's an attempt to create an immersive context which, upon closer inspection, is little more than a theatrically staged set of aggressively cropped images meant to create an indelible impression of Real Life or Drug Trafficking or

Parked Cars in The Rain. This is not science. This is not even design. This is artifice.

Hegel once posited an inevitable transition of thought, brought about through contradiction and reconciliation, formed along a trajectory of thinking that began from an initial conviction and evolved to its opposite. In the thesis/antithesis/synthesis model of Hegelian dialectic, we easily locate the scientist, who migrates from observation to analysis to discovery. Meanwhile, the designer catalogues the everyday, making thick, wordless books with pictures that jump the gutter.

0.007. Nomenclature

Design has always built its discourse upon the languages of parallel professions. Ours is an eclectic lexicon drawn from literature and architecture, from painting and film—disciplines which, arguably, belong in the same broadly-defined cultural orbit, and which, by conjecture, share a certain formal rhetoric. The 1990s rush to transform design vocabulary into the language of branding stems from a similar desire, albeit a commercial one.

Importing terminology from more distant worlds is inherently more problematic. To a certain extent, the success of this dynamic relies on conceptual plausibility. It is one thing to modify a form, another thing altogether to plagiarize an idea. So as objectionable as it may be to stave off the glut of derivative, scientifically-visualized publications that have nothing whatsoever to do with science, it is more egregious, still, to witness the degree to which scientific jargon has been voraciously co-opted along the way. The prevalence of the Lab Book is a case in point. From Fortune-500 annual reports to self-promotional process books lies a plethora of objects and publications with fractional numbers and gridded fields upon which messages are expressed in ScienceSpeak. Posters are pseudo-pharmaceutical and signage is seismic; DNA is all about Group Strategy and periodic tables reduce everything to a cryptic typographic acronym. And this is just the tip of the iceberg. Never before has the nomenclature of science been so misused, overused and abused at the hands of creative people.

And you thought deconstruction was bad.

0.008. The New Vernacular

Designers have long been drawn to the vernacular, appropriating found artifacts and celebrating the texture of the street. Over time, the vernacular became a way to create instant nostalgia, a surface style that looked authentic but was anything *but*. From appropriation came inspiration, a postmodern culture of juxtaposition and pastiche. Because the vernacular belonged to everyone, it resonated as real, familiar and accessible. It was the art of the everyday, beautiful in its ugliness: design within reach.

Faux Science is the new vernacular, a methodology that, while highly disciplined in a formal sense, is still all about appropriation. Arguably, perhaps, the landscape has shifted from street to laboratory. The aesthetic has shifted, too, from grit to grid. It's not so much a tension of form versus content as a favoring of style over substance.

Science represents an enormous opportunity for designers, but not if their contributions remain fundamentally restricted by what they know. At the core of this critique lie serious questions about the role of education. Why don't design students study music theory? Why aren't they required to learn a second language? And why, for that matter, don't they study science? "The difficulty lies not in the new ideas," wrote John Maynard Keynes, "but in escaping the old ones." In other words, design *beyond* reach.

Jessica Helfand and William Drenttel are partners in Winterhouse, a design studio and publishing company in Falls Village, Connecticut. Jessica Helfand's most recent book is *Reinventing the Wheel* (Princeton Architectural Press, 2002). William Drenttel recently published *The National Security Strategy of the United States of America* (Winterhouse Editions, 2002). Their next book is a visual history of the Periodic Table of the Elements.

* Jesse Gordon and Knickerbocker, in: *Speck: A Curious Collection of Uncommon Things*. Peter Buchanan-Smith. Princeton Architectural Press, 2001)

6.26.02:
Cranky

By Rick Valicenti

When I invited Rick Valicenti to contribute to this issue (on June 26, 2002), within
hours I received his "rant," which is printed on the following pages. We did caution Rick
with a brief missive that said: "Hi Rick. Nothing like a spur of the moment genuine rant!
You touch all the bases. If this is really your contribution to No.64, that's allright with
me. No problem for me to run as is, set line for line. I should say, just so you know, that
it will run alongside other people's 'rants' who will spend months thinking about theirs."
Rick wanted me to mention this. RUDY V.

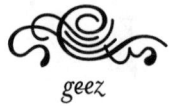

geez

ît's 4:30 am
and I'm typing to Rudy V
  (what the ~~fuck~~ is wrong wîth this pîcture?)

Martha Stewart's ſtock price has dropped 37%
insider trading secrets bubble to the surface

ohmigod
what if Martha goes to jail!

  yikes

is that worse than Winona goin' to jail?

  let's not talk about ît now

there's fires in Arizona
the world is coming to an end
love loſt fires ſtill rage in Colorado
lil' ģirls kidnapped in juſt 'bout every town
other intern's bones found in the park

please, God, I hope we never lose Martha
we love Martha
she is our modern vestal virgin
she made style a good thing
she made simplicity feel right again
she made MFA clean typography from Yale
   mean something
she makes holidays a joy
she captured our spirit for living

   thank you, thank you

I read recently that 6 of 10 Americans are obese
actually they are *only* 20 pounds or more
   overweight

   whew

I'm 20 pounds overweight
but I never considered myself obese

as I watch my weight
I find myself watching the weight of others.

   damn, there's fat ~~fucks~~ everywhere!

everyone has a double chin and saddlebags
or at least 6 of 10 citizens do
big time population growth

and traffic

yikes

so many huge ass cars
(obviously, form follows function)
the contagious seduction of size and style
(a lil' chrome makes 12 mpg seem responsible)

we got it all in this country
America rules...
and good thing we got a President
protecting *our* way of life.
easy money, fast food and fast cars

civilized culture

as for me...
I got game
I am culture
I am designer
I know culture
I forge culture
I lead culture
I speak for culture
I am the form of culture
I am the colorist for culture
I am the wordsmith of culture
I am the typesetter of thought

I am the editor of image
I am the court jester for the king
I am the manipulator
I am the art director
I am the creative force
I am the perfectionist
I am the service provider
I am the seducer supreme
I am the big idea
I am the value added
I am the distinguishing factor
I am the sweet spot
I am the home run
I am the equity
I am the quality control
I am smart choice
I am the right point of view
I am the voice
I am the current style
I am the master of modern
I am what is now
I am new
I am next
therefore:
I am the embodiment of culture

embodiment + 20 pounds, that is

being in this esteemed position…
I delight in the moment and reward myself
  with a fanny pat
for having provided more than my share
of easy fixes to numb our everyday existence,
for being the value added provider
of mindless dribble to sell *more*
  than the competition
for knowing what is the best means of
  manipulating perceptions.
for all those long daze and all nighters,
oh yes, I did take more than one for our team

and looking back…
I simply say thanks for the opportunities
for it was worth every ounce of my energy

  just look at my portfolio

looking down from 30,000 feet
(if I had a dime for everytime
  I heard that bullshit phrase)
I can see that hard work has its rewards.
we can all agree western civilization never looked
  so good
and they want us to believe globalization is right

  glad you agree

in fact, give yourself a fanny pat
you deserve credit too
you are one of us
together, we made everything seem so groovy

you know...
we made logos a real necessity
we made the swoosh ubiquitous
we made branding the holy grail
we made communication a number one concern
we made modernism mod
we made post modernism go away
we made the grunge an aesthetic
we made the internet

sorry, Al

we made the interfaces flash
we made banner ads, too!
we made up the idea of spam
we made annual reports
  society's easy to read/must read bible
we made corporate leaders into rock stars
we put the spin in motion
we made success attainable in our lifetime
we made it all look so easy
we made it all seem so valuable

oh yeah, along the way…
we succumbed to the obligatory focus group testing

will sacrifice evenings for catered cold cuts and cheddar cubes

we digitally enhanced the naughty bits and zits
we dabbled gratuitously in support of sustainability
we provided big time lip service
   on behalf of commerce
we held the sweaty palms of big business
we spelled risk in lower case type
we made fonts popular for everyone
we provided choices to pick from
we created the illusion of customization
we replaced content with messaging
we thought information equaled inspiration
we turned our back on meaning
we stumbled to author real content
we formatted everything
we distilled experience while touting its virtues
we digested all thoughts prior to spitting them back
we fabricated truths when there were only lies
we hypnotized our public with illusion
we raped the street of its character
we appropriated the counter culture
we commodified the artists
we became the great producers
   for not so great product
we felled the forests for advertising's inserts

we covered every surface with die-cut vinyl noise
we silenced the naysayers across the conference
    tables with blah blah blah
we did what we were told whenever necessary
we earned graduate degrees to measure up
we learned to speak in power point
we labeled ourselves in black
we flaunted client lists like badges of honor
we turned some of our own into culture's gods
we let Chairman Mau define life style
we tried to be important
and on our path we rarely said...

  no.

so what do we have to show for all our overtime?
quite a bit actually,
while consumed by the sweet smell of success...
we produced glossy zines showcasing our bounty
    and sweat
we partied mindlessly hard at our national
    conferences
we hid behind well-meaning manifestos
we idolized our own
we became the shit that didn't smell

  'cause we made everything groovy

Now that's the stuff we can all sign our name to

so kick back…
make yourself comfy and ask:
what (the ~~fuck~~) did we really do during our
    professional lives?
what did we do with all those award certificates?
what right answers have we really provided?
what serious problems did we really solve as
    problem solvers?
what difference did we really make?
what wisdom have we really left behind?
what have we really said about ourselves?
what do we make that we can really be proud of?
what have we done to show we really care?
what of our (collective) offering really feels
    enlightened?
what messages have we spread to really insure a
    peaceful spirit?
what goods and services have we aligned ourselves
    with that are good services?
what might our soul really look like?
what image in the mirror should we really believe?

  oops, did I say something to disturb you?

well, we all know:
('cause we told each other and the world through
    the messages we craft)
life's short, play hard
win at all costs

success has its rewards
take no prisoners
ride into the sunset
be all you can be
get to know no boundaries
dive into your pleasure
invest so you can retire
elevate your game

damn

gotta go to a meeting and I'm late
be certain the revisions get out right away
and, wouldya make that call for me?
could ya also do this
and do that
do this
do that
do this
do that
do this
do that

please?

~~fuck~~ you
just do it
ah...
~~fuck~~ this

~~fuck~~ that
no…
~~fuck~~ you
no…
~~fuck~~ yourself
what da ~~fuck~~ did you say?
~~fuck~~ you
no, ~~fuck~~ you, asshole!
take this
take that
eat me

what?
you heard me
~~fuck~~ you
~~fuck~~ off you fat ~~fuck~~

ah, ~~fuck~~ it.

now dontcha feel a little bit better?

6:53 am

(I type with only two fingers)

What's My Motivation?

BY SHAWN WOLFE

"**All that he does seems to him, it's true, extraordinarily new, but also, because of the incredible spate of new things, extraordinarily amateurish, indeed scarcely tolerable, incapable of becoming history, breaking short the chain of generations, cutting off for the first time at its most profound source the music of the world, which before him could at least be divined. Sometimes in his arrogance he has more anxiety for the world than for himself."**

FRANZ KAFKA, *APHORISMS*

MAYBE I'M TOO OLD to still be such a confused lad, but it takes years to become as confused as I feel right now. Only by benefit of hindsight do you get a good look at your own personal ball of confusion as it fills your rear view mirror. A mass of contradiction piled on top of irony, auspicious beginnings tangled up in abandoned or misplaced hopes, shot through with both good intentions *and* ill will, and all of it bearing down —inescapably—on no one but you. You can attempt to go about your business, even *mind your own business*, but objects in the mirror are always closer (and larger) than they appear.

THIS PIECE WAS GOING TO BE ABOUT GUM. Not about gum exactly, but about the recent redesign of the Wrigley's Spearmint and Doublemint gum packaging. And not even about those redesigns specifically, but rather about the reactions those redesigns provoked in me when I first saw them. I didn't get very far with it though. By the time I'd dashed around the neighborhood buying up dusty examples of the old Plen-T-Pak® designs and brought them back to my studio my outrage had waned. As I lined the old Wrigley's packages up alongside the new ones, I realized I just don't care that much. Actually I felt ashamed for thinking it mattered at all in the first place. Indeed, what do I care what Wrigley's does with their legacy brands? In a shitstorm of packaged stuff that I habitually process and track, what is one more American icon down the chute? Besides, wouldn't I be a little bit off my rocker to sit here and bemoan the loss of any one gum wrapper when I can't turn on my television or pick up a newspaper or even talk to anyone anywhere without being reminded that we're, you know, at *war?* The thought that things like pox and nuclear warheads are either going to be in play sometime soon or are at least a "gathering danger" gives one pause. It sobers a person up and throws everything into jarring focus. Not just your work, but your whole outlook on life and history are seen from a strange new perspective. For instance, I'm old enough to know that Doublemint gum hasn't changed noticeably in many decades, but I'm young enough that a World War is something I have no real concept of. So like many of us, I'm really in the lurch here, flummoxed, trying to figure out where I stand. What matters.

Why was I bugged by Wrigley's redesign in the first place? Only now that the old wrappers are gone do I realize that Wrigley was probably the only brand out there (the Hershey bar notwithstanding) that had stood perfectly still and allowed the shifting winds of design trends to just blow over them for longer than I've been alive. I guess I admire that. It's silly, but I'm a designer and I can't help but notice these things. I felt betrayed. I grew up behind my grandmother's candy counter, so maybe I have some kind of unnatural sentimental attachment to gums and candies. (I was similarly perturbed earlier this year when I noticed that the dandy Pringles Guy had been updated for no good reason into some new supercool Pringles Dude with attitude. Just pointless.)

I suppose these new Wrigley's packages are cooler, for what that's worth and depending on your definition of cool. I suppose sales of Doublemint will see some kind of spike. But newness wears off, quickly, and these new designs have nothing to recommend them beyond their newness. Like Franz observed over seventy years ago, there is an incredible spate of new things. A spate! And despite their newness... strike that... *because of their newness* these redesigns are scarcely tolerable, incapable of becoming history.

Not that chewing gum is the stuff of history, but I look around and see very little in the quotidian world that reveres and maintains a link to the past. I think this is why we have nostalgia. The culture cycles through everything so quickly—discarding last week's model to make room for next week's, to keep the wheels of commerce humming ever faster—we're constantly moving on and leaving bits of ourselves behind before we're ready, before we've understood those bits, before we've understood ourselves. So we go back, whether consciously or not, in hopes of piecing together some kind of bridge of meaning. It's not regressive, it's simply the result of rushing headlong into the present, too quickly, and at the expense of reason, as if the future won't wait.

It's only a gum wrapper, and I'm only a graphic designer, but to the degree that consumerism is the lifeblood of our society, these things are little packs and wads of history, by gum. And to the degree that my identity and sense of purpose and self-worth is wrapped up in being a designer of graphics, I can't help but notice and care and feel pissed off when such a simple, utile (practically *undesigned*) piece of the cultural landscape gets suddenly re-landscaped without notice or justification.

It's not like the sky is falling. Change is good. Everything changes. Change puts food on a designer's table. And Wrigley's probably needed to shed that Geritol/Doan's Pills image or die. (Look what happened to Haley's M.O.!) My outrage, if I can call it that, comes from knowing where this is heading. Or how it goes. How it goes around in circles. Two or five years down the road, Wrigley's looks at the intolerable, unhip (i.e., bad) designs they hatched in 2002 and starts thinking back to the "classic" years prior. "What were we *thinking*?" And they resurrect the old package in some form and crow about it and remind us all that they are embracing or bringing back something—for us. It doesn't have to be gum. It could be the Ford Thunderbird, Classic Coke, the NBC peacock. I even recently saw a KFC ad that chirped about a special limited edition "classic original bucket" design they were reissuing as part of some promotion. A curious move after the misstep a few years ago where they reinvented the Colonel as an animated break-dancing jive turkey. (*"GO* Colonel! *GO* Colonel!" Don't tell me you forgot already.)

Never mind the fact that no one's going to be "collecting" greasy cardboard chicken buckets. But these things do come back around, to the extent that brand managers wake up one day and deem it is the right time to remind us that they are not only ever-changing and forever young but also that they have been around since the Hoover Administration.

I should just let it go, but before I do I must say, it amounts to a show of bad faith on the part of Wrigley's, Pringles, Midas, AAA, Burger King or anyone who does a quick hatchet job on their classic trademark. It's bad faith because as consumers we are supposed to care. We're cajoled into caring. We're supposed to be attracted and faithful to these icons. Not that I am a particularly faithful or enthusiastic consumer, but as a designer I have to point out a lousy makeover when I see one. The flying oval Burger King logo just looks desperate and sad. Same with the Midas and Pringles logos. They all spin indiscriminately from the witless spiral school of logo design that was a joke well before 1998 when this all reached critical mass. (see http://www.splorp.com/critique/) Of course I would gladly take the commission myself and would handle any one of these brand face lifts with tender, loving care. But when I see someone else's attempt, particularly when it's worse than the original I just think, "intolerable," "incapable of becoming history," convinced, in my arrogance, that I might have done better. I'm glad someone had a nice payday for their efforts except for the fact that we all have to live with the result cluttering up the landscape.

But again, I'm a confused lad. My priorities are still all mixed up, try as I may to get or keep them straight. Am I mistaking a History Of Commerce—of which branding is a part—for actual History? If so, why should that be? The marketplace (and its proliferating pathogens; brands, ads) is metastasizing, gaining in importance at all levels, causing us to confuse the pursuit with the happiness. My passage to the past, to my personal past, is furnished with gum wrappers and old soda machines and "brandcestors." For me to fret about these facelifts is surely a sign of misplaced or displaced values.

THERE'S BEEN A LOT OF TALK for a long while now—both inside the design world and outside of it—about re-examining what we do, why we do it, where we're heading. A lot of hand-wringing and forehead-smiting. Maybe not enough, but there has been more and more of it in recent years. Enough that it seems to have started to make a difference. The events of the past year or two—starting with the butterfly ballot fiasco of 2000—have caused many of us to look closer at ourselves. Concern about, and awareness of the effects of our actions (and our inaction) have never been higher.

In April of 2002 I had the opportunity to take part in AIGA's *Voice2* biennial conference in Washington D.C. I didn't know quite what to expect. The event was originally scheduled for the week following September 11th. Naomi Klein and Kalle Lasn and myself had been scheduled to appear and talk about branding and adbusting and anti-branding, respectively. Neither of those two appeared at *Voice2* though, and going into it I felt my talk about "Life At The Point Of Sale" was, in light of recent events, a bit off topic. Possibly even in poor taste.

The mood at the conference alternated between positive, ponderous, joyous, and grim. The speakers were inspiring and the energy among the attendees was invigorating. But I think everyone, myself included, felt a new added weight of history, of life and death, bearing down. Not one word was spoken about design trends. At least not in the sense of how things *look*. None of that mattered. All anyone wanted to talk about was the reason for a design, or a photograph, or a publication. Stripping the profession down to essentials, peeling off layers of fashion and pretense and getting to what mattered. "What's my motivation?" was the muffled mantra I heard myself and everyone else muttering to themselves for three days. It's a question I've been badgering myself with pretty much every day since I emerged from design school. I can't leave it alone.

I'm pretty sure I decided to go into design because I thought it would be fun. I didn't think it through all that much. I didn't know from motive. I just knew I liked it. I had an eye for it and had probably been gearing up for a career in design before I knew that's what I was doing, when it was still just play. Like many of us, when the time came to choose I chose a line of work that I had a passion for. That was all I had to go on at 17. I cared what stuff looked like. Still do. And that was enough to sustain me through art school and into the early years of my career. It *was* fun. It *was* exciting. I remember when just seeing galleys come back from the typesetters was exciting. Then seeing something in print. That was exciting. Getting paid to do it was icing on the cake. But soon enough, too soon, it started to get unexciting. Four years down the road I was losing interest. Or I should say, I was losing interest in the kind of design I was doing. In retrospect, I see that I was in the early stages of a full-blown Crisis of Meaning. I didn't understand it at the time, but I had a nagging sense of it. I didn't trust my nagging senses in those days though. I figured the problem was me. I was a malcontent, unable to feign interest in what he was doing enough to continue doing it. I was too young at the time to be feeling burned out. And perhaps "burned out" is overstating things. But silly questions like, "Is *this* all there is?" and "Why *bother*?" came up regularly. Stern voices in my head would answer back: "This isn't supposed to be fun, Shawn. That's why they call it work."

Or I would console myself with the words of my old boss from Retail Planning Associates, "Doesn't this beat working?" by which he meant that design, even the design of modular point-of-purchase signage systems for pet food chains, still beats the hell out of manual labor. And maybe it does.

But my gripe wasn't that I wanted to not work. I grew up with a work ethic. I didn't shrink from the effort and the toil (or even the frustration and compromise) that are part of the creative process. But these normal work stressors had begun to wear on me. My eye, on more than a few occasions and for days on end, twitched uncontrollably, all on account of some *faux* distressed jeans tags and embroidered heraldic crests that signified nothing. And that's pretty much how I've come to think of my life from the years 1987 to 1993: "SOME *FAUX* DISTRESSED JEANS TAGS AND EMBROIDERED HERALDIC CRESTS THAT SIGNIFIED NOTHING." The fact that they signified nothing—no history, just some borrowed and mangled symbols of counterfeit status—was insult enough. But the volume of work was numbing. The rote churning out of similar *faux* distressed jeans tag designs and heraldic crests and shields and chevrons over and over again, and made-up ski resort matchbook art and fake country clubs and phony-baloney cricket teams, "authentic" fly fishing "outfitters" gradually snuffed out whatever passion I once had. This work became something not just to agonize over and complain about, but also to apologize for. It was no secret that these goods were being produced by little hands in offshore work camps. And all of it was on its way to a Salvation Army drop box in eighteen months' time anyhow. Something to bear in mind when assessing one's self-worth.

Whatever pleasure I may once have taken in art or design—or surrealism, for that matter—was trounced by this exhausting pursuit of nothingness. I felt dirty for helping create those graphics, for helping to contrive that patina of *fake authenticity*.

I didn't care about history *per se* back then, but I cared about futile exercises. And I cared about design. About doing good work. And the work I was doing, I eventually realized, wasn't worth caring about. It wasn't even design, so how could it be good?

Eventually I decided that I needed to get out and find something that was worth doing. Work that mattered. I wasn't particularly interested in politics or causes. I wasn't going to run off and apply to the Sierra Club, although around this time it was not unusual to read accounts of other designers and ad men who were doing just this. "Dropping out"... "Reassessing"... I was reassessing too, but I was thinking along more self-interested lines. Joe Campbell's "Follow your bliss" was whistling in my ears like a teakettle. "One life to live." "Preference... because I'm worth it." "Just do it." That sort of thing. Heeding this call seemed even riskier than just switching from The Limited to Greenpeace. Because, well... what *was* my bliss? Why did I consider graphic design a good career choice in the first place? The answer was I loved it. Originally. But it was the early 90s already, and... like... *where did the love go?* Could I plod ahead without it even if I wanted to? If so, *should I?*

But my love of design, as I had known it, had turned into something else. I was taking new pleasure in *using* design, not just to perform on the job and pull down a pay check, but to articulate rage. *My* rage, such as it was. To give myself a voice that was as loud, as smart, and as self-important as I could devise to make it seem with the aid of a Macintosh. Raging was becoming popular, anyhow. Not just in music and film but also in graphic design. I set *my* sights on branding but there was also raging going on against legibility and against the page. Whether these were bouts of conscience or a case of designers simply waking up and casting about for some better, other, or new use of their talents, it amounted to a re-examination of what we do, how we do it, and why.

Teeth-gnashing and rule-breaking were going on both in the profession as well as at its edges. It led to culture-jamming as we've come to know it. It led to renewed interest in media studies. To the D.I.Y. movements in small press and indie publishing. And it led to designer-initiated projects like Beatkit and Obey. Desktop publishing (and later the Internet) heightened the powers a designer could wield and gave him or her unfettered access to an audience that would not have existed or been within reach only ten years prior.

The Crisis of Meaning had already reached a boiling point when the Internet boom hit. Soon design and illustration and animation and video and journalism were all melted into one, oozing out the other side as a kind of e-fodder, as *content*. While the economy ballooned during the latter half of the decade, instances of design seemed to proliferate like so many holes to fill or surfaces to resurface. The new millennium itself could serve as justification for a quick makeover. Nothing went untouched or unstyled. Everything is dressed cool now. Ketchup, cell phones, Band-Aids, computers. Virtually nothing you come in contact with has not seen its edges beveled, has not been smothered in trendy graphical sauce or shaped into a blueber-ry teardrop, or, ultimately, flattened completely. Design is more than just cool now. Design is popular. Design is mainstream. Even your mom knows what a font is. And she has her favorite. And that's where it's at.

Oh, and we're at war.

THE WORLD IS CHANGED. But much of what was normal before is still normal. Designers were already finding and using their voices, were using the tools of their trade to *say something*, were questioning what they did, were learning to appreciate the role they played, the responsibility they bore for creating the cul-ture. Not just visual culture or pop culture or consumer culture but, because these things have been allowed to become our real-ity and our reason to live, *THE* culture. And that's exciting. It can be and often is a lot of fun. But it's also a big responsibility when it comes time to infuse our work with values, with mean-ing, and with worth. Designers can use design to articulate big questions and raise awareness. Or they can use it to amuse themselves to death. I've been guilty of both.

The biggest challenge of all is the challenge we've had all along, namely, solving problems. The culture industry is all too efficient at spitting out new things of no significance or nutri-tional value, manufacturing an intolerable junk culture that often seems incapable of becoming history. Can this be resis-ted? Can it be changed? Improved upon? Maybe it is arrogance talking (or what's left of my passion) but to this designer's way of thinking the biggest problem facing us is the problem of maintaining the chain of generations. It's a problem of coherence, of meaning, of divine signal versus amateurish noise. And if that doesn't motivate, I don't know what will.

Shawn Wolfe is best known as the man behind the anti-brand Beatkit™ and the RemoverInstaller™. A monograph of his design and illustration, *Uncanny* (Houston/Gingko), was published in 2000. In 2002 he worked with Jelly Helm and Mark Barden on "AWAKE," a campaign to promote The Center For A New American Dream. CNAD is a non-profit organization that advocates reducing consumption and shifting consumer behaviors. Wolfe designed the organization's identity as well as a series of street posters on the theme of "AWAKE."

It's Back!

WE ARE HAPPY TO REINSTATE the always popular Readers Respond section. Your comments to our publication never stopped coming, but due to limited space in the past four issues we've had to save them up. We are publishing them here.

As always, we're curious to know what you think. Send your comments to: editor@emigre.com or mail a letter to Emigre, 4475 D Street, Sacramento, CA 95819, USA.

RVDL

Dear Emigre,

If the "manifesto" *First Things First 2000* contained the same type of thinking that your column [in *Emigre* #56] did, I can understand why it was viewed with such skepticism.

There is as much of a need for us to "save the Earth" as there is a chance that we could destroy the Earth. The Earth has been around for about 4.5 billion years. It has survived the impact of natural phenomena that man cannot dream of creating. The Earth and its resources were here long before us—and they will be here long after us.

Though well intentioned, the cry to "save the Earth" is silly thinking or sloppy communication. Which is ironic, for if we are to achieve the meaningful goal of better utilizing the Earth's resources that we value, sound thinking and effective communication will be essential.

Calling our society "waste-based" is inaccurate and counter-productive. Our society is based on families and individuals. Our economy is based on supply and demand. Our governments are based on republicanism and democracy. Understanding the three and their distinctions is essential to effecting change on a large scale.

As long as individuals have the awareness, freedom, and incentive to inspire our families, friends, and neighbors, the private sector and public sector will respond.

Individuals in a market economy have the greatest opportunity to bring about change. Though more is needed, the evidence is abundant—there are recycling centers for your wife to use because the market (people) wanted it. McDonalds stopped wrapping their hamburgers in styrofoam because of market pressure. The list goes on and on.

Conversely, how many things can you name that a majority of consumers have demanded that the market did not make available?

Better use of the Earth's resources will come with increased availability of three human resources—awareness, freedom, and incentive. I applaud your intentions and your wife's extraordinary efforts. I look forward to trying on my first pair of Patagonia shorts.

Mathew Higbee

Dear Emigre,

Congratulations on an outstanding issue #59. It seems like the first time *Emigre* writers have taken up the social/political/commercial/capitalist controversy without sounding like they are whining. I was this close to ending my subscription (indeed, #59 was my last issue), but you've redeemed yourselves. Great discussions, involving both primary data from the "marketplace" and analysis of the complex problems and choices we are faced with. Thanks, and I hope you'll keep up the great work.

Sean Walter

Dear Emigre,

Hello, gentlepeople! Jelly Helm's words on page 70 of Rick Poynor's article in *Emigre* #59 hits home with: "There are features about advertising—some kinds of advertising—that are emphatically not points in a gentleman's game. The major part of the activity is honorable merchandising, without taint. But there are projects that undertake to exploit the meaner side of the human animal—that make their appeal to social snobbishness, shame, fear, envy, greed. The advertising leverage that these campaigns use is a kind of leverage that no person with a rudimentary sense of social values is willing to help apply..." – W.A. Dwiggins, *Layout in Advertising* (1928)

If we rise above the mechanics of our brains and see that what each of us does affects all humanity and the planet, we might get the feeling that each word, each design has both short—and long—term consequences. Regard each human we affect as special and we might come to our senses of what we are becoming, and what we might become.

Thanks for getting us to use our minds a little more than we have been. Nonetheless, our spirits and our souls are the message, not the media!

Regards,
Frank Gaude

Dear Emigre,

I just received your latest issue (#59) and started into Chris Riley's, "Sustainable Consumerism." Very good so far. I looked across the pixelated images of beer bottles and related them to the list on the previous page. The fact that I knew they were bottles of *beer* is scary enough. But is noticing that some are not listed in the right order a testament to "branding"? Did you bastards do it on purpose to see who'd notice and prove the article's point?! Hmmm... it might also be I worked in a supermarket and was exposed to them every day... nah.

In any case, I believe #3 Lowenbrau is actually the 10th bottle, #13 Guiness is the 15th, #15 Grolsch is the 18th, #18 Budweiser is the 14th, and if there are any others I am not familiar with them... yet. Keep up the excellent work.

Dave Beasley

Dear Emigre,
This is my story. In 1991 I discovered your magazine. Wow! My

blood pumped, my heart filled, my ears pricked. Design was now cool. I committed myself to design, feeling it was a unique blend of artistry and message. Years later this feeling began to fade. I felt angry and ripped off. The world doesn't want creativity and passion, I thought. I started to hate design; it was nothing more than corporate business, computers and money. Where was my soul? Where did my passion go? I started to ask myself these questions. I had blamed the world over and over for my dying interest, until I became tired enough.

A few years ago, after trudging through some deep depression, I committed myself again, but this time to honoring creativity— to let it guide me. It has brought me back to life. In truly connecting with my creative spirit, I have come to respect every communication I have. I am grateful for each and every client, and this is what matters for me. Through my clear communication, trust, and creativity, I am able to help many realize their dreams with the design I provide them. This service actually makes a difference. By transforming my "business" into a spiritual practice, I now uplift people to be who they truly are— happy and whole. In return my life is full of joy. I am doing artistic work that touches people. Design and spirituality are now cool.

I am grateful for you being a part of this process.
Thank You
Christopher Lawrence

Dear Emigre,
I'm positively impressed. The Spring 2001 issue is subversive, ideological, and incorrect. We need more!!!
Fernando Diaz Najera

Dear Emigre,
Issue #60 is stunning in its simplicity, in its form and in what I feel is a return to form for *Emigre*. As of this evening, after I walked in and picked up the mail, the only issue I treasure more is my Designers Republic issue (*Emigre* #29).

Standing in my front hall, holding it in my hands, before I even had the poly off, I was moved by what you had done. Design is Good. Design is Powerful. You've renewed my sense of purpose in what I do. What we do. With my sincerest thanx for doing what you do so well for so long and for the extremely generous free ride you let me take.

Chris Aguirre

Dear Emigre
Thank you for the Honey Barbara CD (*Emigre* #60)! I could not believe my ears when I first heard it—that I actually liked a random CD sent to me in the mail. And now, not only do I simply like it, I've got to have more! It is amazing to me that a group so talented and original is so underground. Their lyrics are a continual source of amusement and awe, and the tone and groove of the instruments and vocals make you feel so funky. I haven't stopped listening to it yet!

Thanks.
Traci Hix

Dear Emigre,
I am so happy with what I received in the mail today. *Emigre* #60 brightened my uneventful day of work. You know how the same routine can get to a creative. Well now I have something in my greedy little hands (greedy, 'cause I'm not circulating this to anyone for quite a while). It's exactly what I needed, wanted, and thrive on.

Emigre, you make me dance in my seat! Thank you!
Beth Wood
P.S. I have lemon-yellow underpants too.

Dear Emigre,
I just finished listening to your CD (*Emigre* #60), and I have been returned to a place that was lost within me—an independent strain of creativity that I muffle in professionalistic facades from day-to-day. The compositions were full chroma. I can't wait for

my next road trip—I need new speakers for the Bug. Wow. You're so beautiful.

Kindness,

Barb

Dear Emigre,

Kudos and high praise for the new format! Long live the chap book! We have been reading *Emigre* since issue four and have enjoyed watching the character and format of the magazine change with time. Keep up the good work.

Lance and Ann Miller

Dear Emigre,

What a fantastic CD (Honey Barbara's I-10 & W. AVE., *Emigre* #60)! Well written, played and produced, more loops than one could shake a stick at. Many thanks to Mr. Sidlo & Co. Some strange stuff goin' on down in San Antonio, a hot-bed of loopdom. Cowboys, loops, go figure.

Mark Sottilaro

Dear Emigre,

I have subscribed to *Emigre* since its inception. Excellent, provocative design and art. I just wanted to say thank you for the last free issue with the music CD. It is much appreciated and the CD is very worthwhile. *Emigre* magazine and its related items is a one-of-a-kind enterprise that truly is something special.

Thanks for the knowledge and memories. Sincerely,

Brian Pirman

Dear Emigre,

Bravo! You folks are just great. Just got your newsletter (*Emigre* #60). I so appreciate your innovation (fun design), your generosity (thank you for the CD), and your consciousness of our planet. You bet I'll buy more type from you. You're a world class act, all around. A peaceful holiday to all,

Virginia

Dear Emigre

Just wanted to preemptively say (i.e., before the critics get started), I think the decision to charge for subscriptions is more than reasonable—especially with the regular buyer's clause. In filling out the questionnaire, I have always stated that I would be willing to pay, and my position remains the same as the move becomes reality. It would be terrible for such a great publication to be the source of monetary loss for *Emigre* (like in the case of such greats as *Critique*). I hope that the additional funds will allow for a bit of further investment in this inspiring and long-standing project. With the creative expertise that emanates from your work I'm sure I won't be disappointed.

David Holman

Dear Emigre,

Just wanted to tell you how much I absolutely love the new CD by The Grassy Knoll (*Emigre* #61)! It's so good I could belch with happiness! Thank you for the inspiration and the classic cool that is "Emigre."

Matt Woolhouse

Dear Emigre,

Thanks so much for your recent edition, and the wonderful music CD (The Grassy Knoll). This band is absolutely sublime. How can I get more of their music?

Thanks again.

Bill Groshelle

Dear Emigre,

First, I'd like to thank you for your recent Font/Music promotional mailer (*Emigre* #61). It's refreshing to see people giving away free "cool" stuff to define their brand. Your earthy recycled stock gives a nice first impression of texture and substance.

However, I fear that while your promo package is well intended, it may totally miss the mark with a large portion of your intended audience. I found the catalog (and basically all of your previous promos) rather abstruse, and only the very last section was of any use with regard to delivering info to my font-hungry brain. Really, step back and look at it. What is your message here? Are you trying to elevate my consciousness, sell me a font, what? Too much information. It all seems a little forced and certainly jumbled. As I deal with fonts in my career as a creative director, I would be intensely interested in anything that can clearly help me find a font with a flavor to suit a particular look or purpose, without distracting me from my creative vision. Simply put, a collection of PDFs (on a CD) that showed me your complete or latest collection of fonts presented in a few varied design and text examples would be very useful. I could print it out, for instance, or put it on the network as a resource. I think it should look a little more like maybe Adobe designed it instead of Das Unterleben Unterground. It should look a little more coherent. Think fresh! I'm not saying you can't have a little fun, just keep it coherent and try to appeal to a wide range of tastes and applications. A good reality check would be to include a little postage prepaid card asking people to rate and comment on your promotions. Alternately, you could invite a random (large) assortment of art directors and designers to a focus group featuring your promotions and catalogs.

Now, the CD!

Nice try. I have the very same kind of equipment in my basement too. Really. I can appreciate your efforts. I think maybe you should look around at your local music scene (young and old) and put together a "something for everybody" CD. Our local music scene has such greats as Taj Mahal (older) and, say, Dow Jones and the Industrials, or the Cappuccino Jellybeans (younger). All these bands are great and I'm sure your local indie artists would jump at the chance to be featured on one of your CDs.

Good luck and my best regards,
Steve van Schouwen

Dear Emigre,

Anyone who missed the boat with The Grassy Knoll's 1998 release *III* gets a second chance with your elegantly presented *Happily Ever After* (*Emigre* #61). If you're into the likes of Lemon Jelly, A Quiet Revolution, Tortoise or Medeski, Martin & Wood, you'll dig it. Great audio presentation, great visual presentation. Nice job, Emigre.

Richard Osborn

Dear Emigre,

I'm guilty of treating your magazine like junk mail.

A while back I had to purchase Mrs Eaves for a client—another design firm had spec'd it along with a batch of custom-mixed ink colors (which our client didn't want to pay for) so I wasn't really happy to be shopping. When the first magazine came to me, I figured it was the first in a deluge of direct mail I would be getting, not unlike the reams of paper I get from Corbis. I tried the first disk I got and it seemed unfriendly to my Mac. (Probably due to my impatience, but whatever.)

It got tossed. So did the next couple of issues.

Today, however, is Friday, and I'm having a party tonight, and my projects for the day are largely done, so I stuck *Happily Ever After* into my computer and read through your magazine.

Now I'm sad that I was clueless.

Thanks for the good stuff.

Stephanie Mitchell

Dear Emigre,

I just received your Spring 2002 issue (*Emigre* #62) along with the *Catfish* DVD, and I wanted to say "thank you very much."

I'm a graphic designer who graduated from SCAD about 3 years ago. Since then I've worked for what I see to be a stuffy corporate advertising agency which has taught me lots but has given me little room to express. Super frustrating. I still create on my own but what I do on a daily basis can hardly be considered art.

Reading the introduction to *Catfish* at the beginning of your magazine, where it talks about Elliott Earls, was inspiring. I don't mean that in a cheesy way, but it seemed to put a little wind in my sails and let me know that many feel and go through many of the same obstacles artistically and professionally that piss me off. I'm not sure I said that properly, but copywriting is definitely not my area of expertise.

Anyhow, thanks a bunch for continuing to provide so many with so much.

Ben

Dear Emigre,

I just watched *Catfish* (*Emigre* #62), and have been playing the "Home Shopping Network" spoof segment over and over—it's by far one of the funniest things I've seen in a long time! In these scary times, that's "worth" a hell of a lot to me.

Crazy, inspiring stuff.

Best,

Kevin Grady

Dear Emigre,

I love getting my mail when *Emigre* is in the box. It makes my week. I look forward to hearing more of the old critical insight from *Emigre*, but wish *Emigre* can keep on with the format of the last four issues—it feels like we've only got started here. If there is any way—anything, additional superhuman subscription, hypnotism, or whatever—by any means continue on this track. It's become a conversation better than anything being said on the shelf or newsstand. Much thanks for the good times. Can't wait to find out what's next. Still soaking in Seattle.

Ben Nechanicky

Dear Emigre,

Hi. I bought issue #63 of *Emigre* today: *The Acid Gospel Experience*. I bought it at the best bookstore and theater in Guelph, Ontario, Canada (The Bookshelf). It was with the magazines, and it sort of looked like one. But it looked like a really wicked CD case too. And so it was. This is cool. It's all cool. You guys should be proud of what you made.

I've seen these little *Emigre* creations before, but I sort of disregarded them because I didn't want to have to think about what they might be. That's never a good idea.

So today I tackled my fear, and the feeling that I should know exactly what I'm buying before I buy it. Anyway, it's here with me now, at home, playing on the damn computer, filling the house with sound. A magazine that plays in the damn computer.

Before coming home I went to the weekly meeting of the ensemble of improvised music, which is held on Tuesday nights in room 107 of the Music Department at the University of Guelph. I opened up the magazine/CD on top of a grand piano. It was cold and cloudy and people were studying for midterms and things, so there was a small turnout. But the people who were there came over and asked about your creation. They were all impressed. A magazine that plays. (Please excuse us for being so impressed— Canadians are easily impressed by things that look like they've come from the heart, the heart of America, the hot and cold desert heart.)

So then I put the magalbum away and we played our weird music. We played in room 107 for a while, then listened to a re-cording made by three people in an enormous water tank with a 40 second delay time on any sound—the most beautiful reverb ever. We were impressed by that too. We were so impressed that we attempted a reverb session of our own, in a nearby stairwell. And holy shit it was wicked. Vocal overtones, cymbal scrapes, clarinets, a violin and gongs. We were great for a few moments.

But I'm home now. I'm sitting at the computer, typing this, reading the booklet occasionally, and listening to soundscapes I've never heard coming from the speakers. Some of it reminds me of the stairwell. Some of it reminds me of other things. I like it a lot.

I read in the introduction that Bruce used to make his own album packaging, and is a renowned designer of CD packages and things. I read that Bruce's work inspired the creation of Emigre

Music. Well, both you turkeys have inspired me.

I don't know anything about CD packaging, but I know when something kicks ass. I don't know much about music either, but I try to make the best stuff I can in the best ways that I know how. I think that what you've made is great music and great packaging, great notes and words, pictures and recycled paper. Great art.

I want to do what you do. I'm trying to start up a record label and, so far, the packaging issue has been on my mind as much as the music, and all the damn computer stuff.

OK. So I'd like to make stuff like you make so one day you might walk into your local music store and buy a book of music that has a little balloon and a little label on the back that says "promispherecords." That would make my day.

I hope this e-mail makes your day.

Sincerely,

Ryan William Neptune Carley

Dear Emigre,

In order to fulfill the eligibility requirements and receive a complimentary new format *Emigre* subscription, I ordered a bunch of sale-priced back issues. After delightedly devouring these old jumbo-format *Emigres*, I was ineluctably led to the following irrefutable conclusion: *Emigre* is shrinking.

Best regards,

Jeff Beamer

Typeface Index:

To order these
typefaces please visit
www.emigre.com

COVER | Fairplex | DESIGNED BY ZUZANA LICKO
AaBbCcDdEeFfGgHhIiJjKkLl

HALF-TITLE | Dalliance | DESIGNED BY FRANK HEINE
AaBbCcDdEeFfGgHhIiJjKk

TITLE PAGE | Mrs Eaves | DESIGNED BY ZUZANA LICKO
AaBbCcDdEeFfGgHhIiJjKkLlM

TITLE PAGE VERSO | Vendetta | DESIGNED BY JOHN DOWNER
AaBbCcDdEeFfGgHhIiJjKkLlMmNn

DEDICATION | Solex | DESIGNED BY ZUZANA LICKO
AaBbCcDdEeFfGgHhIiJjKkLlMmNnOoPp

& Dalliance | DESIGNED BY FRANK HEINE
AaBbCcDdEeFfGgHhIiJjKk

CONTENTS LIST | Fairplex | DESIGNED BY ZUZANA LICKO
AaBbCcDdEeFfGgHhIiJjKkLl

INTRODUCTION | Filosofia | DESIGNED BY ZUZANA LICKO
AaBbCcDdEeFfGgHhIiJjKkLlMm

PAGES 15-34 | Vendetta | DESIGNED BY JOHN DOWNER
AaBbCcDdEeFfGgHhIiJjKkLlMmNn

PAGES 35-44 | Eidetic Neo | DESIGNED BY RODRIGO CAVAZOS
AaBbCcDdEeFfGgHhIiJjKkLlM

PAGES 45-56 | Cholla | DESIGNED BY SIBYLLE HAGMANN
AaBbCcDdEeFfGgHhIiJjKkLlM

PAGES 57-72 | Fairplex | DESIGNED BY ZUZANA LICKO
AaBbCcDdEeFfGgHhIiJjKkLl

PAGES 73-84 | Fairplex | DESIGNED BY ZUZANA LICKO
AaBbCcDdEeFfGgHhIiJjKkLl

PAGES 85-98 | Mrs Eaves | DESIGNED BY ZUZANA LICKO
AaBbCcDdEeFfGgHhIiJjKkLlM

PAGES 99-113 | Los Feliz | DESIGNED BY CHRISTIAN SCHWARTZ
AaBbCcDdEeFfGgHhIjKkLlMm

Emigre script logo
designed by John Downer.

PAGES 114-126 | Filosofia | DESIGNED BY ZUZANA LICKO
AaBbCcDdEeFfGgHhIiJjKkLlMm

State of Graphic Design

A Visual Essay

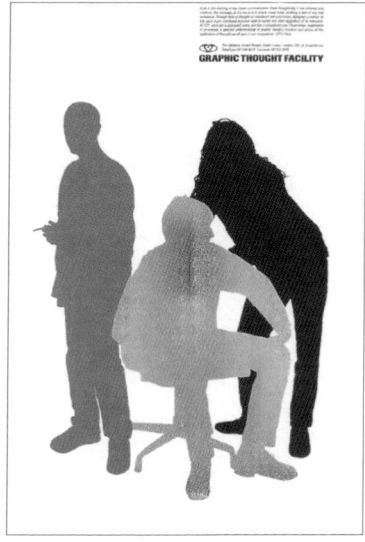

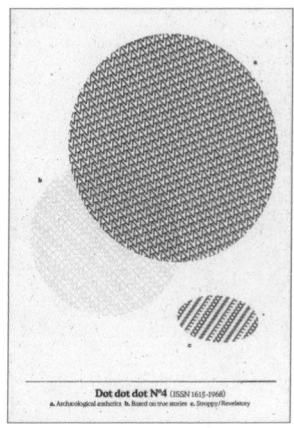

Dot dot dot Nº4 (ISSN 1615-1966)
a. Archeological esthetics b. Based on true stories c. Stroppy/Roselency

Left: Self-promotional poster,
by Graphic Tought Facility.

Above: Cover design for
Dot Dot Dot No.4, 2002,
by Stuart Bailey and Peter Bilak
with Goodwill.

Below: Diagram for sound
composition, by Daniel Eatock
of Foundation 33.

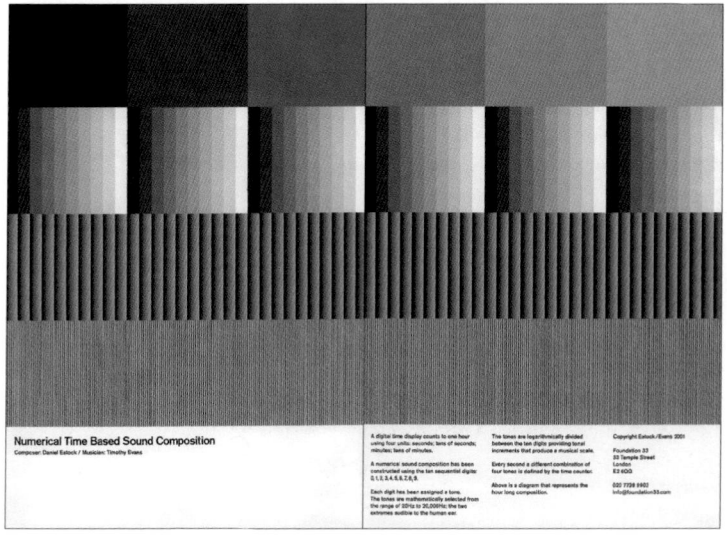

Numerical Time Based Sound Composition
Composer: Daniel Eatock / Musician: Timothy Evans

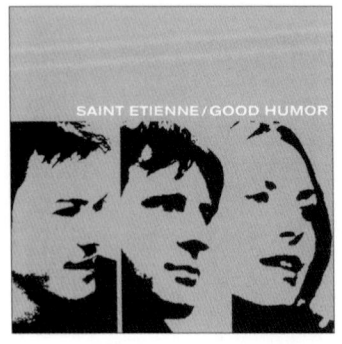

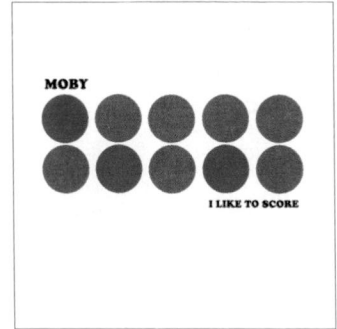

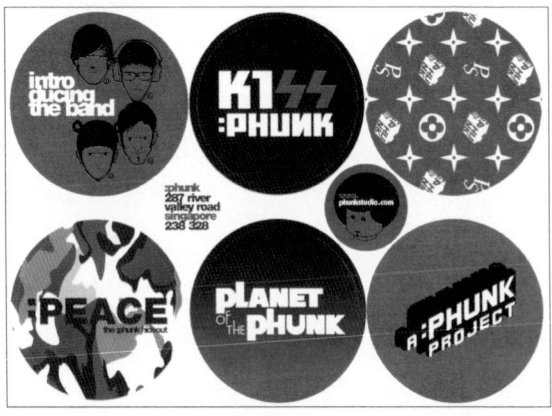

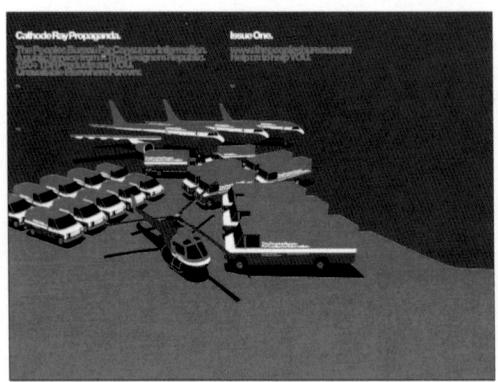

Top to bottom:

Saint Etienne,
Good Humor,
CD cover by
Phantom Industries.

Moby,
I Like to Score,
CD cover by Alli.

Sheet of stickers
by :Phunk.

*Workforce Desktop
Wallpaper*. Free down-
loadable propaganda
from The Designers
Republic website.

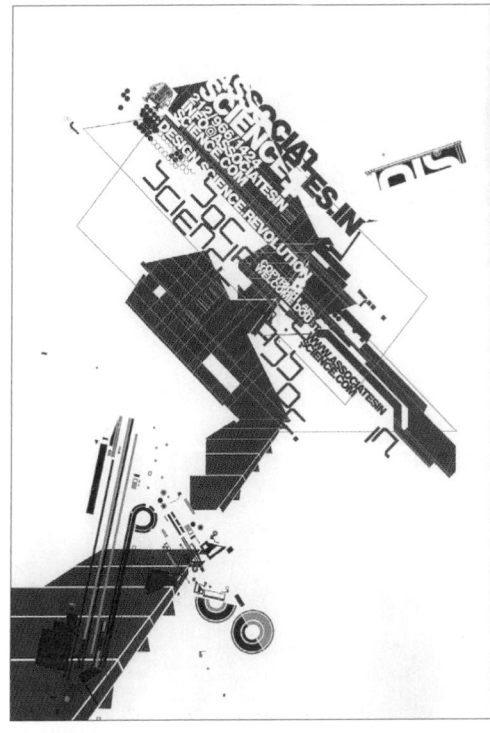

Left: Design by Associates in Science. From the book *Coast to Coast: Contemporary American Graphic Design*, Die Gestalten Verlag, Berlin 2002.

Below: Spread from *Enjoy Survive/Survive Enjoy*, by Olaf Nicolai and Norm, Die Gestalten Verlag, Berlin, 2002.

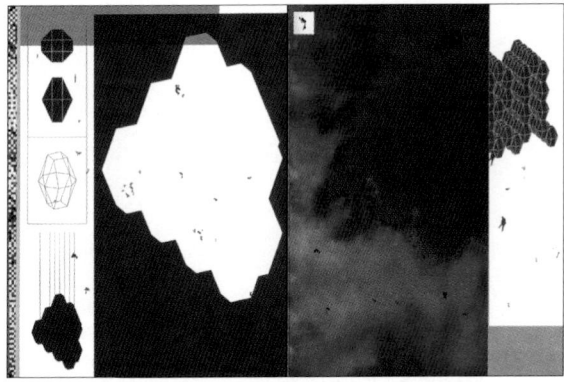

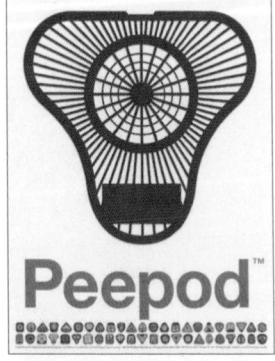

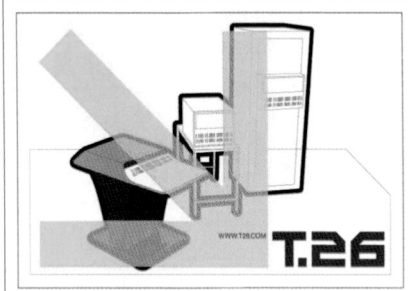

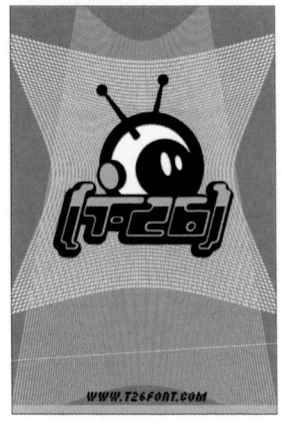

Above: Various
promotional materials
for the digital type
foundry T-26.

Left: Molecules,
*England, Ireland and
Scotland, also including
North America and
Wales.* CD cover by
Stuart Bailey.

Importado por: M. Mexico
S.A. de C.V. S.J. de Aragon 516
07070 Mexico, D.F.
Hecho en: E.U.A.

Cinta magica/magic tape

Disappears when you apply it,
stays invisible
Can be written on; long lasting
Fits most dispensers

This is the 2x4 web site in which you will find an introduction to the personnel; samples of our projects (including branding and identity systems, advertising and web sites, posters, collateral materials, books, brochures and catalogues, magazines, film and video, environmental graphics and exhibition graphics); a list of the artists, musicians, galleries, museums, architects, and all-around smart people who are our clients and collaborators; various essays and articles; information about the Museum of the Ordinary; an empathy exam; a curious collection of evidentiary material of questionable origins; a messy area dedicated to work in progress, unfinished projects, rejected ideas, unresolved concepts and other things that don't quite seem ... eople we like; pictures of our studio; an ... ind us, how to see more work, how to ... oking for a job.

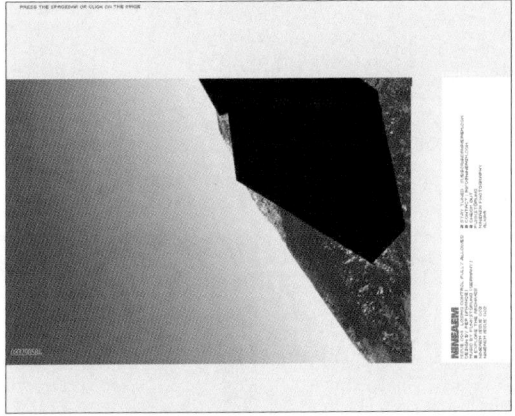

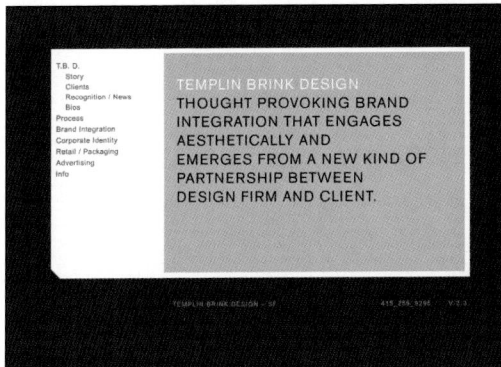

Top to bottom:
Website designs,
www.2x4.com
www.nineaem.com
www.templinbrinkdesign

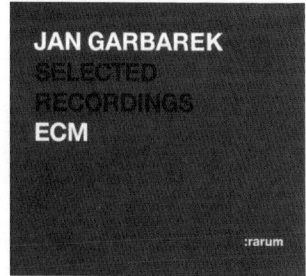

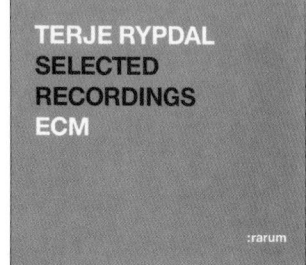

Above: Advertisement for *All Tomorrow's Parties* CD, designed by Ben Drury.

Top & bottom right: Jan Garbarek, *Selected Recordings*, Terje Rypdal, *Selected Recordings*, from the ECM :rarum series, CD covers designed by Manfred Eicher.

Right: Page spread from the book *NoiseFour*, designed by Attik. Gingko Press, 2001.

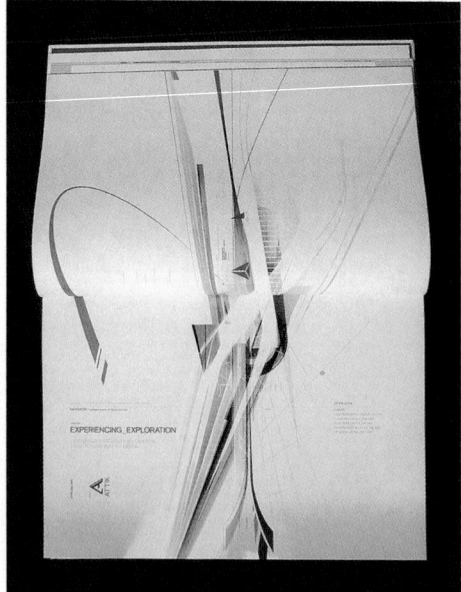

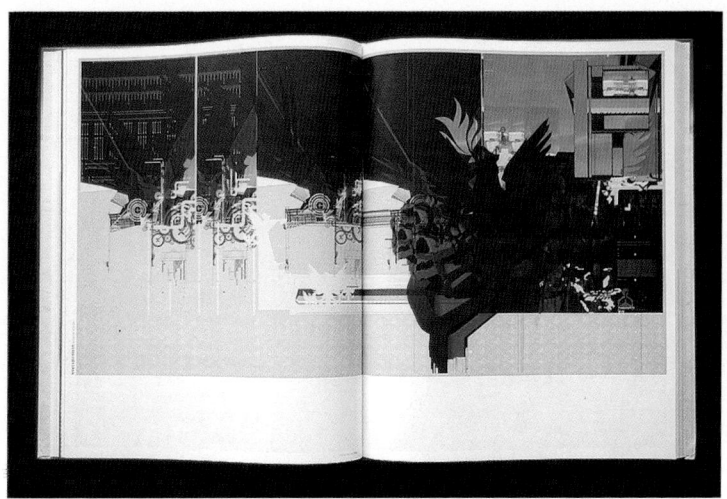

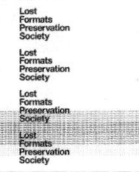
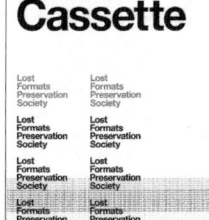
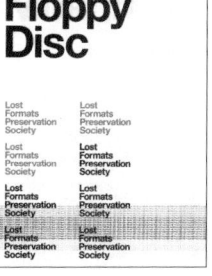
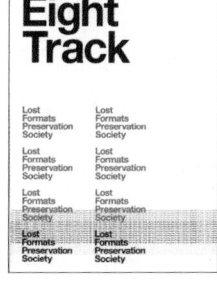

Top: Design by WeWorkForThem. From the book *Coast to Coast: Contemporary American Graphic Design*, Die Gestalten Verlag, Berlin 2002.

Above: Six of seven cover designs for *Emigre* No. 57, 2001, by Experimental JetSet.

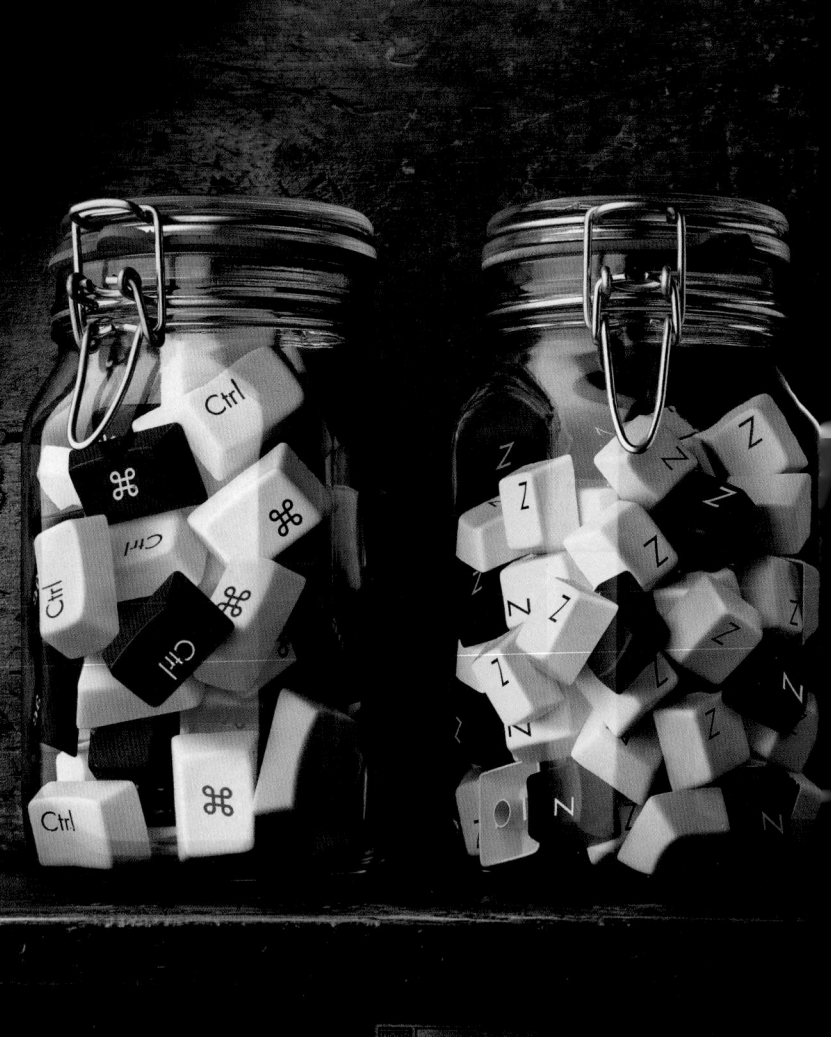

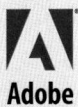

Adobe

Multiple undos. Because bad things happen in threes.

Or fours, or fives. But, luckily, it doesn't matter.
Because with our unlimited number of undos and redos you'll be
able to return your file to the happy place it once was.
To learn more, take a test drive at www.adobeindesign.com.

| Adobe InDesign 2.0 | Tools for the New Work: |

HELLO

WE'RE PRINCETON ARCHITECTURAL PRESS.

WE PUBLISH BEAUTIFUL AND STIMULATING
BOOKS ON ARCHITECTURE AND DESIGN.

LIKE THE ONE YOU'RE HOLDING IN YOUR
HANDS. *RANT, EMIGRE #64.*

WE'RE VERY PROUD AND EXCITED TO
BE THE OFFICIAL CO-PUBLISHER AND
DISTRIBUTOR OF *EMIGRE*.

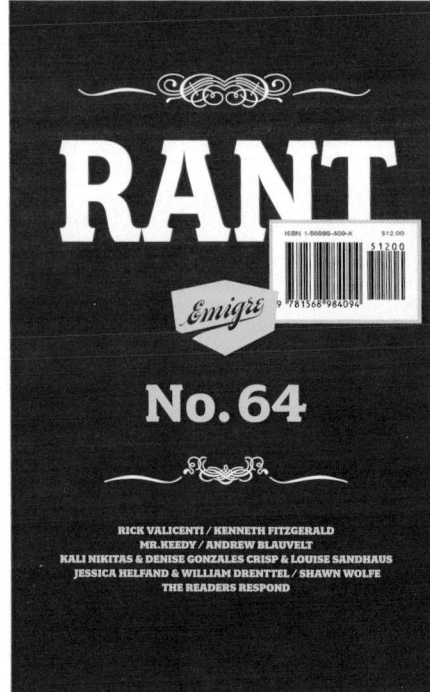

RANT

Emigre

No. 64

RICK VALICENTI / KENNETH FITZGERALD
MR.KEEDY / ANDREW BLAUVELT
KALI NIKITAS & DENISE GONZALES CRISP & LOUISE SANDHAUS
JESSICA HELFAND & WILLIAM DRENTTEL / SHAWN WOLFE
THE READERS RESPOND

ISBN 1-56898-409-X $12.00

HERE ARE SOME DETAILS THAT MIGHT INTEREST YOU:

BEGINNING WITH *EMIGRE #64*, BOOK RETAILERS
AND WHOLESALERS WORLDWIDE WILL BE ABLE TO ORDER
EMIGRE FROM US OR FROM ONE OF OUR DISTRIBUTION
PARTNERS OVERSEAS. SIMPLY CONTACT OUR NEW YORK
SALES OFFICE AND ASK TO SPEAK WITH THE SALES MANAGER:
212.995.9620, X208 OR EMAIL NETTIE@PAPRESS.COM

IN THE COMING MONTHS WE'LL BE PUBLISHING OUR NEW LIST OF TITLES IN DESIGN.

COMING APRIL 2003

HELLO WORLD: A LIFE IN HAM RADIO DANNY GREGORY AND PAUL SAHRE
6.5 X 9 256 PP 500 COLOR 1-56898-281-X PAPERBACK $24.95 £16.99 €29 SFR 45

INSIDE DESIGN NOW: THE NATIONAL DESIGN TRIENNIAL DONALD ALBRECHT, ET AL.
8.5 X 11 208 PP 400 COLOR 1-56898-394-8 HARDCOVER $50.00 €60 SFR 88
1-56898-395-6 PAPERBACK $29.95 €36 SFR 54
FOR SALE THROUGH PRINCETON ARCHITECTURAL PRESS IN NORTH AND SOUTH AMERICA, AND ASIA ONLY

DESIGN FOR IMPACT: FIFTY YEARS OF AIRLINE SAFETY CARDS
ERIC ERICSON AND JOHAN PIHL 9.1 X 12 176 PP 136 COLOR 1-56898-387-5 PAPERBACK $30.00
FOR SALE THROUGH PRINCETON ARCHITECTURAL PRESS IN NORTH AMERICA AND THE PHILLIPINES ONLY.

COMING MAY 2003

BRODSKY AND UTKIN: THE COMPLETE WORKS LOIS NESBITT
9 X 12 128 PP 83 DUOTONES 1-56898-399-9 HARDCOVER $45.00 £30.00 €54 SFR 82

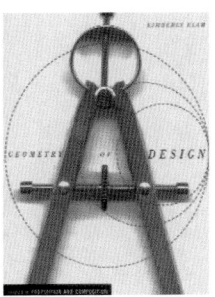 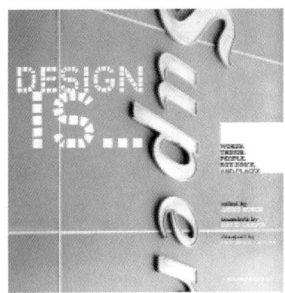 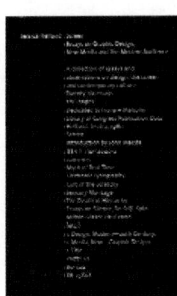 

GEOMETRY OF DESIGN
Kimberly Elam
8.5 X 7
96 PP, 4 COLOR, 92 BW
1-56898-249-6 PAPERBACK
$14.95 £10.95 €18.50 SFR 27.50

"EVEN IF YOU ALREADY KNOW THAT MIES VAN DER ROHE'S BARCELONA CHAIR WAS WELL PROPOR-TIONED, THE NIFTY TRANSPARENT OVERLAYS IN *GEOMETRY OF DESIGN* CAN PROVE IT....EDUCATES THE READER AND BRINGS THE DESIGNS TO LIFE."
—*NEW DESIGN*

DESIGN IS...
Akiko Busch
8 X 9.6
288 PP, COLOR THROUGHOUT
1-56898-314-X PAPERBACK
$29.95 £21.95 €36 SFR 54

"NO MATTER WHERE THE READER PLUNGES IN, SOMEONE IS SAYING SOMETHING PROVOCATIVE OR BRILLIANT, FASCINATING OR INFURIATING."
—*MODERNISM MAGAZINE*

SCREEN: ESSAYS ON GRAPHIC DESIGN
Jessica Helfand
5.25 X 8
208 PP, 500 COLOR
1-56898-310-7 PAPERBACK
$19.95 £13.95 €24 SFR 37.50
1-56898-320-4 HARDCOVER
$45.00 £30 €54 SFR 82

"DESIGNERS WHO WRITE ABOUT OTHER DESIGNERS ARE A RARE BREED. RARER STILL ARE THOSE WHO WRITE WELL. HELFAND IS JUST SUCH A RARITY. AS BOTH A PRECISE, JARGON-FREE ANALYSIS OF THE STORY OF 20TH CENTURY DESIGN AND AN INSIGHTFUL GUIDE TO ITS PROGRESS IN THE 21ST, HELFAND'S THIRD BOOK IS A COLLECTION OF SOME OF HER SHARPEST OBSERVATIONS ON MODERN VISUAL CULTURE."
—*FACE*

WHAT IS A DESIGNER?
Norman Potter
5 X 8.25
184 PP
0-907259-16-2 PAPERBACK
$20.00 AVAILABLE FROM PRINCETON ARCHITECTURAL PRESS IN NORTH AND SOUTH AMERICA ONLY

"POTTER'S GREAT ACHIEVEMENT IS TO FASTEN UNERRINGLY ON THE TRUE NATURE OF DESIGN, AS A SERIOUS ACT OF INTELLECTUAL ENQUIRY WHICH INVOLVES MIND AND HEART AND NO PRECONCEPTIONS. THOSE WHO STILL BELIEVE IN THE IMPORTANCE AND DIGNITY OF DESIGN WILL CLUTCH AT IT LIKE A LIFEBELT."
—*BLUEPRINT*

FOR MORE INFORMATION ON THESE AND OTHER TITLES, PLEASE VISIT OUR WEBSITE AT WWW.PAPRESS.COM

Mrs Eaves

OPENTYPE®

SUPERMARKET

NOTES ON THE MOJAVE DESERT. WORDS AND IMAGES BY RUDY VANDERLANS. A GINGKO PRESS BOOK.

SCALE

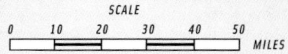

0   10   20   30   40   50
MILES

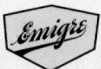

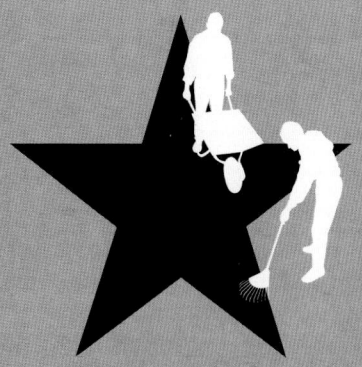

Emigre Product Info

Emigre Magazine
U.S. 4-Issue Subscriptions: $28.00
Foreign 4-Issue Subscriptions: Canada $35.00 / Elsewhere $58.00

Back Issues
Many back issues are available at the regular cover price.
A limited number of collectors' issues is available at $50.00 per copy.

Free Catalog
To order a copy of the Emigre Fonts Catalog go to:
www.emigre.com/EmigreCatalog.html or call us at 1.800.944.9021

Books About Emigre
A number of books have been published about the work and history of
Emigre; **Emigre (the Book): Graphic Design into the Digital Realm** (now in
its 5th printing!), gives an overview of the founding of Emigre in 1984 and
covers the first 10 years. $50.00; **The Emigre Exhibition Catalog** was
published as part of the Charles Nypels Award which Emigre won in 1996.
$8.95; **50 Questions 50 Answers** is an interview with Rudy VanderLans
presented in small book format. It was published on the occasion of an
exhibition of the work of Emigre in Istanbul, Turkey in 1998. $5.00

Emigre Music
Over the past 12 years Emigre Music has released 23 CDs; from Basehead's
Play With Toys (voted by *Spin* magazine as one of "The 90 Greatest Albums
of the 90's"), to the recent inclusion of Scenic's latest CD, **The Acid Gospel
Experience,** in *Emigre* #63. On our website you can download free MP3
samples of Emigre Music releases and read interviews with the musicians.

miscelaneous
Emigre also offers T-shirts, artists' books, posters, wrapping paper,
mousepads, and the always popular Sampler Bag containing a collection of
Emigre goodies.

Mailing List
Help us keep our email and mailing lists up to date. You can change your
email address, or take yourself off our mailing list at:
http://www.emigre.com/work/acct_login.php

How to Order Emigre Fonts & Products

Order On-line

www.emigre.com
This is the most convenient way to order and you'll avoid
font shipping costs. Fonts are available for immediate
download, all other items are shipped within 3 business days.

Order by Phone

Call 9-5 Pacific Standard time.
Charge your credit card.
Phone: **916.451.4344** or **800.944.9021** within the US.

Order by Fax

Print out a faxable order form at:
http://www.emigre.com/EFax.php
Fax anytime: **916.451.4351**

Order by Mail

Enclose payment by check or charge your credit card.
All checks must be payable through a US bank, in US dollars.
Mail to:

Emigre
4475 D Street
Sacramento
CA 95819
USA

Emigre News

Add Yourself to the *Emigre News*
emailing list. We use *Emigre News* to
help keep you informed of new
products, services, and special limited
offers. To sign up go to:
www.emigre.com/enews

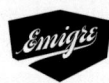

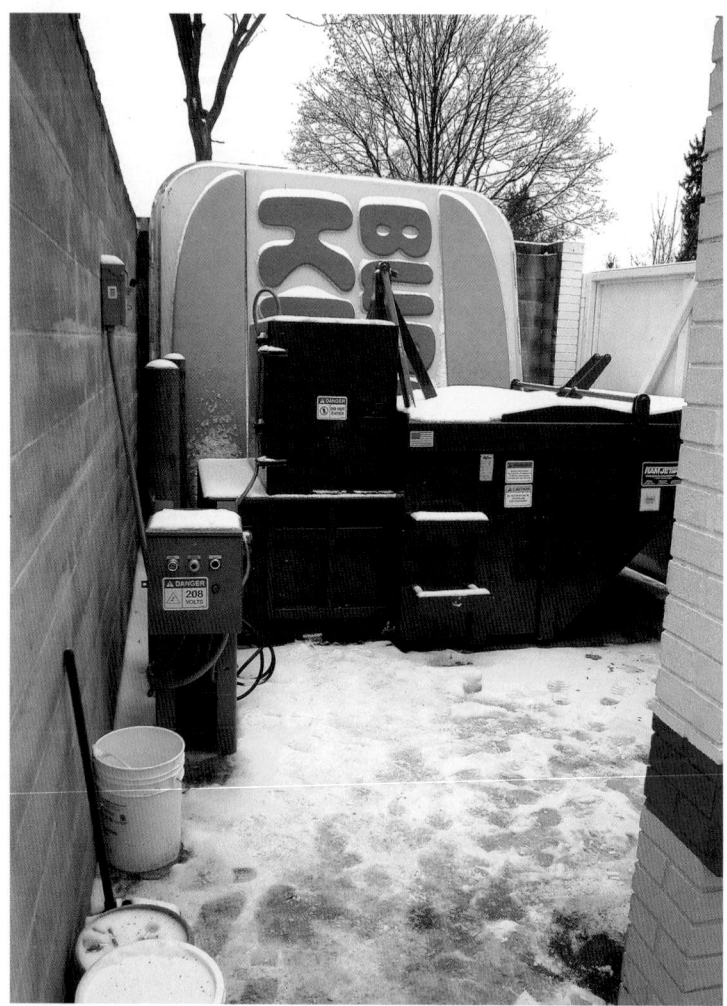

PHOTOGRAPH BY SHAWN WOLFE.

"In a shitstorm of packaged stuff that I am habitually
processing, what is one more American icon down the chute?"
– Shawn Wolfe, *What's My Motivation?*, Page 99.